Gyles Shute

The Antidote to Prevent the Prevalency of Anabaptism

clearly vindicated from that foul aspersion of being a counterfeit, and the aspersors totally confuted: or, another broad-side against Anabaptism

Gyles Shute

The Antidote to Prevent the Prevalency of Anabaptism
clearly vindicated from that foul aspersion of being a counterfeit, and the aspersors totally confuted: or, another broad-side against Anabaptism

ISBN/EAN: 9783337298210

Printed in Europe, USA, Canada, Australia, Japan

Cover: Foto ©ninafisch / pixelio.de

More available books at **www.hansebooks.com**

THE ANTIDOTE

To prevent the Prevalency of

Anabaptism

Clearly Vindicated
From that

Foul Aspersion

Of being

A Counterfeit,

And the

ASPERSORS

Totally Confuted:

OR,

Another Broad-side against ANABAPTISM.

By *Gyles Shute* of *Lime-house.*

LONDON,
Printed by *J. R.* and are to be Sold by *Nathaniel Hiller* in *Leaden-Hall-street*, *William Chandler* in the *Poultrey*, *Samuel Norcut* at *Stepney*, *Will. Wingod* in *King-street*, *Wapping*: *James Wright* in *Shadwell*, near the Church; and at the Authours House in *Lime-house*. 1694.
Price bound One Shilling.

The Antidote to prevent the Prevalency of Anabaptism clearly Vindicated from that foul Aspersion of being a Counterfeit, and the Aspersors totally Confuted.

I. HERE is *a Reply to Mr. Hercules Collin's Book, which he saith is an Answer to my Book, Intituled,* An Antidote to prevent the Prevalency of Anabaptism, *&c.*

II. *Here are some Remarks upon several Positions I met with in a late Book of Mr.* Benjamin Keach's, *which I cannot pass without taking some notice thereof.*

III. *and* Lastly, *Here is an Answer to several Assertions, and very strange Positions, which some Persons of their own Opinion did Declare to me on the Second of* June, 1693. *in* London, *in a Conference I had with several of them about Infants Baptism.*

First I shall begin with Mr. *H. C.*

Sir, I have read your Book, which you are pleased to call *The Antidote proved a Counterfeit,* and you say it is an Answer to my Book, Intituled, *An Antidote to prevent the Prevalency of Anabaptism, or Infants Baptism Vindicated,* which I do own my self to be the Authour of the said Book: It was not that I was ashamed to own it, that I did not put my Name to it, but I did not then think it convenient so to do; but I find you have made a very lame, imperfect Answer unto it, notwithstanding I believe you have exercised the best of your own skill, with the assistance of others; but I find your Stile is very unbecoming a Minister of the Gospel, as you profess your self to be; it doth not at all favour of a meek Frame and Temper of Spirit, but of a proud, lofty, supercilious Frame and Temper of Mind, as if you thought to bear down Truth before you, and to drown it with your reproachful, scornful Words, and opprobrious Language, more like a Turk than a Gospelized Christian; and what you your own self are guilty of in your Book, you charge me with in mine, therefore I will refer them both to the Judgment of any Impartial Reader: But I bless God I can bear all your Reproaches and Calumnies chearfully, and it shall no ways discourage me, nor hinder me from vindicating the Truth, and contending earnestly for the Faith once delivered to the Saints.

And I will not render Railing for Railing, but what I have to offer in Vindication of Infants Baptism, and the Everlasting Covenant God declared and made with *Abraham*, I shall labour to declare in the Spirit of Meekness, onely sometimes

times you muſt expect a gentle Touch, to put you in mind how groſly you have abuſed me, and in ſome things, where it cannot be avoided, but I muſt grate a little ſmartly upon you, there you muſt bear with me, although I ſhould accoſt you in the moſt ſenſible Parts, becauſe otherwiſe I cannot vindicate the Honour and Glory of the Grace of God, nor my own Credit and Reputation.

1. I find you have omitted ſeveral Material Points in my Book, and paſt them by without taking any notice at all of them.

2. You have charged me falſely in ſome things.

3. How you have boggled and juggled with the Sacred Scriptures, as ſhall be made evidently appear.

I find the Sum and Subſtance of your whole Book wrapt up and contained in the Preface thereof, which is the Foundation of all your Florid Arguments in theſe Words following;

1. *Here thou haſt the Cavils and Objections of the Adverſary anſwered.* 2. *Infants or Little Children proved to have no Habitual Faith* 3. *The Deſolution of the Old Covenant State demonſtrated.* 4. *And the Infants of Believers to have no Right as the Seed of ſuch to Holy Baptiſm.*

On theſe Topicks are all your Arguments and Deductions built againſt us Pædobaptiſts: So that to Anſwer theſe Four Things, is to Anſwer your whole Book.

You ſay that you were dead to the Anſwering of my Book a long time, and truly, Sir, give me leave to tell ye, you have made but a dead Anſwer unto it at laſt, and I ſhall take care to bury it.

But however it will paſs for a full Anſwer to my Book, with thoſe that are ſo horribly bigotted to their own Opinion, as that they durſt not read mine, nor contradict yours; but what ſaith *Solomon* of ſuch, *The ſimple believeth every word, but the prudent man looketh well to his going.*

Firſt, Say you in Pag. 2. *The Right Mode of Baptiſm is by Dipping:*

But I think there is more to be ſaid for ſprinkling, or pouring Water on the Face in Baptiſm, then there is for Dipping or Ducking over Head and Ears in a River or Pond: For the latter is more like a puniſhment of Criminals, then the Solemnizing of an Ordinance of God. Pray hear what the Scripture ſaith of Sprinkling, and of pouring Water upon Sinners to cleanſe them, *Heb.* 12. 24. *And to Jeſus the mediatour of the new covenant, and to the blood of ſprinkling,* &c. 1 *Pet.* 1. 2. *Elect according to the foreknowledge of God the Father, through ſanctification of the Spirit unto obedience, and ſprinkling of the blood of Jeſus Chriſt.* And *Iſa.* 44. 3. *For I will pour water upon him that is thirſty, and flouds upon the dry ground: I will pour my ſpirit upon thy ſeed, and my bleſſing upon thine offspring.* Ezek. 36. 25. *Then will I ſprinkle clean water upon you, and ye ſhall be clean: from all your filthineſs, and from all your idols will I cleanſe you.* Exod 24. 8.

Here you ſee we do not read of Dipping nor Ducking in all thoſe Spiritual, Metaphorical Baptiſms, which are all nearly related unto the Ordinance of Baptiſm, and tend to the ſame thing, but more effectually and perfectly, and are accompanied with the ſame Promiſes, namely, the Remiſſion of Sins, Sanctification by the Spirit, and the Gift of the Holy Ghoſt, compare with *Acts* 2. 38, 39.

Secondly, We do not find that there was either River or Pond of Water in the Jaylor's Houſe, for himself, and all his Houshold, to be Dipped or Ducked under Water in; for they were all Baptized in the same hour of the Night, in which they were Converted. Indeed if it had been at an Inn, something might have been said more to the purpose; for we find, that many of the Inns in *London* have Ponds in their Yards, to wash their Horses in; but it is dangerous for a Jaylor to have a Pond in his House or Yard, for fear left any of their Prisoners, in a Fit of Despair, should drown themselves. Pray let us hear what the Scripture saith in *Acts* 16. 29, 30, 31, 33. *Then he called for a light, and sprang in, and came trembling, and fell down before Paul and Silas.* The occasion of this you may see in the Four foregoing Verses: *And he brought them out, and said, Sirs, what must I do to be saved?* Pray take notice, the Jaylor did not say, what must I and my Houshold do, but what must I do to be saved? Mark the Apostles Answer unto him, *And they said, Believe on the Lord Jesus Christ, and thou shalt be saved, and thy house. And he took them the same hour of the night, and washed their stripes; and was baptized, he and all his, straightway.*

1. Here you see they were all Baptized in his own House.
2. In the same Hour of the Night.
3. They did not go out of the House to a River.
4. We do not read of any one Soul of them that did believe, besides the Jaylor himself, before they were Baptized, nor of any one Act of Faith they exerted.

Mr. *Sidenham*, Page 93.

It's not a slight thing to consider, how that ever since the Fall this hath been an usual Method of God

in Administration of the Covenant, and
of Grace, to make it run through F
Housholds of Believers, as the special l
Families, as they were the first natura
they were the first Churches; and when
in Abraham's time came to be more e:
and fairer expounded, God goes on stil
Method, makes the Covenant with A
his Houshold, &c. Now if you come to
stament, there you see God going on in
thod, as if he had cast by an Eternal
Platform. Baptism, the New Testamei
is administred according to the same des
lies and Housholds: Consider what (
saith to Zaccheus, Luke 19. who wa
and one of the chief Publicans, upon oc
Mans Conversion, to open the nature an
of the Covenant to the Gentiles, in t
as it was to Abraham, This day is sa
to thy house, forsomuch as he also is
Abraham. Assoon as ever he was co
believed, Christ applies the Promise to
If there were not something more in
have only said, Salvation is come to the
is the son of Abraham, is as much as
Priviledges of the Covenant is the san
your House, as it was to Isaac and Jaco
as he also is a Son of Abraham, as
And to tell them of their Housholds, a
to them in the Beginning of the Gospel
the same time exclude their Infants from
signs of the Promise, which they ever
darkest Days of Grace, is a strange Poli
to the simplicity of Jesus Christ. The
with a gracious Entail, Acts 11. 14. C
the Promise to him, and his House; Lyc
tized, and her House; the Apostle exhor

to believe, and he should be saved, and his whole House. Just as God made the Covenant with Abraham, Walk before me, and be thou perfect, and I will be a God to thee, and thy seed or houshold, *Gen.* 17. 1, 2, 7.

Where whole Houses are baptized, their Infants are not excluded, if they be in the House, and if not excluded, they are included; they cannot be excluded, for they are principal Parts of the House; and if only Adult should be meant when Children are named, that would be to exclude Infants from being Children, as well as from being Parts of the Houshold. Thus Mr. *Sidenham.*

Joshua said, *As for me and my house, we will serve the Lord*, *Josh.* 24. 15. Here he was resolved upon it, and solemnly ingages, that he and all his, would serve the Lord, that was himself and all his Children: Let others take what course they will, if they will not serve the Lord, I cannot help it, I am sorry for it, but I and mine will serve the Lord; I know that I and mine (as if he should have said) are in Covenant with the Lord, and therefore we will serve the Lord; he would so demean himself towards his Children, both by Examples, Instructions, and Corrections too, as that they should serve the Lord visibly, if not spiritually and internally: For if the Head of the Family be a Believer in Christ, then himself and Family maketh a little Church comparatively, 1 *Cor.* 7. 14. And as all that are of a visible Church, may not be Elected, and therefore not Saved, so neither may all be Elected and Saved of such a Family or Church, no more than *Judas* was, who was baptized, and one of Christ's own Family, though a notorious Hypocrite, and bloody Traytor.

What were all these Persons that *John* Baptized? (1.) Will any Man affirm, that they were all Believers? (2.) Will any Man prove there were no Children amongst them all? Though Mr. *H. C.* will not allow, that there were any in the Jaylors Family; And for an Invincible Argument to prove it,

1: Saith Mr. *H. C.* in his former Book, pag. 33. *Whereas some say, No doubt but the Jaylor had Children, It may be very much questioned, seeing it hath been observed some Years agoe, that for very many Years together, not one Child was born to the Jail-Keepers in all the County of* Essex.

But what is this to the purpose; if he could have proved, that never any Jail-Keeper in *England* had ever had any Children, it had been more to the purpose, yet that would not have made his lame Argument crawl upon all Four, unless he could have proved, that all the Jail-Keepers in the World, never had any Children, but lay under a perpetual Curse of Barrenness, Entailed upon that Office. Pray, Sir, who is guilty of Non-sence now?

But to proceed, Pray do but take notice of those Persons that came to be baptized of *John*, and see how many Believers there can be found amongst them,

2. Whether it was possible that there could be no Children among them all; for it is said, *Then went out to meet him Jerusalem and all Judea, and all the regions round about Jordan, And were baptized of him, confessing their sins,* Mat. 3. 5, 6.

1. If Children were not included, then it could not be all and every Individual Person.

2. If

3. Take it in which of the [Alls,] you pleafe, and you will not find, that Little Children can poffibly be excluded.

But perhaps you will fay by all that Country, as you have faid of the Jaylors in *Effex*, That there was no Children among them, which may as well be faid, there are none in all *England*.

2. It may be objected, How could young Infants confefs their fins? It may as well be queried, How could thofe little Children make a Covenant with the Lord in *Deut.* 29. 11, 12, 13.

3. It may as well be faid, How do Godly Minifters confefs the Sins of the People; and do we never read of Parents confeffing the Sins of their Children; and do not Gofpelized Minifters confefs the Original Sins of young Babes, when they baptize them; for they do, or ought to do at leaft wife, baptize them, confeffing their Sins; and pleading the Promifes for them, as in *Acts* 2, 38, 39. And do we not hear and fee Bills fpread before the Lord, almoft every Lords Day, in the publick Affemblies by Parents, confeffing the Sins of their Children. In ver. 7. *But when he faw many of the Pharifees and Sadduces come to his baptifm, he faid unto them, O generation of vipers, who hath warned you to flee from the wrath to come? Bring forth therefore fruit meet for repentance* &c, ? Who were viler Perfons than thefe? Yet *John* baptized all that came unto him of the natural Seed of *Abraham*. We do not find, that he refufed, or turned away any; for we read, that all were baptized of him:

But he baptized none of the Gentiles, becaufe
the

the Blffieng of *Abraham* was not yet defcended upon them. *John* Baptized them upon the ſame Topick which they were Circumcifed on, which was by vertue of their being in that everlaſting Covenant God made with *Abraham*, which alone gives fufficient Authority to believing Parents, to baptize all their Children in their Infancy. *John* told the Jews, they muſt not think to fay, *Abraham* was their Father, that will not ſerve your turn; for if you live in Sin, and indulge your felves in Wickedneſs, and die in that condition, it is not *Abraham*'s being your Father can fave you; for you may hear one of *Abraham*'s Sons a praying to him in Hell; whether he was a Jew or a Gentile, or whether it was a Parable, I cannot tell; but let him be who he will, *Abraham* could not help him to fo much as one Drop of cold Water to cool his ſcorched Tongue withal. There was no more Indulgence or Liberty to Sin under the Law, then there is now under the Goſpel; but the Soul that finned muſt die: God would by no means acquit the Guilty then, neither will he do it now, *Exod.* 34. 7. *Joſh.* 24. 19, 20.

But I do believe, that there were more Modes in Baptiſm than one; for fome went down into the Water, and others were baptized in their Houfes; but I cannot underſtand, that any were Ducked all under Water; it is poffible their Faces might be Dipped without plunging the whole Body under Water, or by pouring Water on their Faces.

Now I challenge you to produce but one poſitive Command, or but one Example, to prove, that ever any Woman went down into a River or Pond to be Dipped or Ducked all under Water in Baptiſm, throughout all the Book of God, or elſe take your *Human* Invention to your ſelf, and

lay

lay your Brat no more at our Door; for it belongs to you, and not to us. Every Sinner that God the Father draws to Chrift, muft come to him naked, without any covering of his own; he muft not appear in his own filthy Rags, but muft come ftript of all, ftark naked: So it muft be in Baptifm, that part of the Man, Woman, or Child, that is to be baptized, muft be naked; wherefore the Face of Man is the moft comely part, and that by which both God and Man are defcribed, *Pfal.* 51. 9. *Pfal.* 84. 9. *Matt.* 18. 10. *Gal.* 1. 22. How common is it among Men to fay, I never faw fuch a ones Face, that is, he never faw the Man. And if it be no Baptifm, unlefs the part baptized be naked, then if the whole Body muft be Dipped or Ducked under Water, it muft be all naked; and what a Reproach would fuch an unfeemly Practice have been upon the Chriftian Religion, at the firft Plantation of the Church among the Heathens, for Women to go down naked into the Water before Men, or in a Shift, to be baptized, by which they become an Object to draw Mens Lufts forth after them, inftead of folemnizing God's Holy Ordinance of Baptifm, and fo inftead of glorifying God, they gratifie the Devil. What was it that proved fuch a dreadful fnare unto *David*, a Man after God's own Heart, but the fight of a beautiful *Bathfheba* wafhing her felf?

And what would an unbelieving Heathen have faid to his believing Wife, that was young and beautiful? Would he not have been prone to charge her with the fin of Uncleannefs; for the Heathens were very apt to charge the Chriftians with that fin, in that Day, without any fuch ground of fufpicion, as Womens expofing their nakednefs to the view of Men.

But

But the Apostle saith, Let all things be done decently, and in order; but I am sure there is no decency in this Practice; and what the order of it is I leave to the Reader.

Pray hear what Mr. *Baxter* saith to this in his Book, Intituled, *Plain Scripture Proof of Infants Church-Membership and Baptism,* in chap. 13. pag. 136, 137.

' My seventh Argument is also against another
' Wickedness in their manner of baptizing, which
' is their Dipping Persons naked, as is very usual
' with many of them, or next to naked, as is
' usual with the Modestest, that I have heard of,
' against which I argue thus, If it be a breach of
' the seventh Commandment, *Thou shalt not com-*
' *mit Adultery,* ordinarily to baptize the naked
' then it is intolerable wickedness, and not Gods
' Ordinance; but it is a breach of the seventh
' Commandment ordinarily to baptize naked;
' therefore it is intolerable wickedness, and not
' Gods Ordinance. All the question is of the
' minor, which is evident thus, The seventh
' Commandment forbids all Incitements to Un-
' cleanness, and all immodest Actions; but to
' baptize Women naked is an immodest Action,
' and an Incitement to Uncleanness; therefore it
' is there forbidden.'

' To this Mr. *T.* made me this Answer in Con-
' ference, That in former times it was thought
' no Immodesty, to which I replyed,

' 1. Custome in some Countries, like *Brasile*,
' or other Parts in *America*, where they go still
' naked, may make it seem no Immodesty there;
' but among those that are not Savages methinks
' it should.

' 2. If Mr. *T.* could baptize naked all the
' Maids in *Bewdeley*, and think it no Immodesty,
' he

'he hath loft his common Ingenuity and Modefty
'with the Truth.
' 3. Is not every good Man fenfible of the de-
' ceitfulnefs and wickednefs of his own Heart,
' and that he needs all the helps againft it; and
' is it not his daily bufinefs to watch over it,
' and his Prayer and Endeavour, that he be not
' lead into Temptation? And would it be no
' Snare or Temptation to Mr. T. to be frequently
' imployed in baptizing Maids naked? Let him
' fearch and judge: Methinks the very mention-
' ing of it (could I avoid it) is Immodefty. So
much Mr. *Baxter*.

2. The Anabaptifts make a great deal of pud-
der and ftir about the Apoftles Words in *Rom.* 6.
and have preft them into their fervice, the words
are as followeth, *Therefore we are buried with him
by baptifm*: They will have it, that this refpects
burying in the Water over Head and Ears in Baptifm; and therefore they make it an Argument
for Dipping. The Apoftle feems to have been
ftirring them up, and putting them in mind of
their Baptifmal Vows and Obligations: It may be
as well to the Children of Believing Parents,
that were grown up, as to themfelves; for in
Ver. 3. faith he, *Know ye not, that so many of us as
were baptized into Jefus Chrift, were baptized into his
death?* That is, as they were baptized into all
the Priviledges, that were purchafed by the death
of Chrift, fo they were baptized alfo into the
fufferings of Chrift; for they were obliged, by
their Baptifmal Covenant, to take up their Crofs
and follow the Lord Jefus Chrift, whitherfoever
he went; and fo are all Chriftians under the fame
Obligation now, by their Baptifmal Covenant.

3. Our Saviour Chrift called his own Sufferings

his

his Baptifm, and a bloody Baptifm it was too; *Luke* 12. 50. *But I have a baptifm to be baptized with, and how am I ftraitned till it be accomplifhed!* Now the Apoftle draws this Argument from the Premifes in Verfes 4, 5. *Therefore we are buried with him by baptifm into death: that like as Chrift was raifed up from the dead by the glory of the Father, even fo we alfo fhould walk in newnefs of life. For if we have been planted together in the likenefs of his death: we fhall be alfo in the likenefs of his refurrection.*

Here is Duty and Priviledge joined together: The Apoftle was exciting them to prepare for Sufferings, which they met with daily, and tells them in effect, that if they did partake of Chrifts Sufferings, which was their Duty, they fhould partake of the Benefits of his Refurrection; if they fuffered for him, they fhould reign with him: There was their Priviledge.

4. You may fee here, that the Apoftle hath joined Circumcifion the Type, and Baptifm the Antitype together, in this Burial of Chrift; and Circumcifion is firft in order, in thefe following Scriptures,

Col. 2. 10, 11, 12. *And ye are complete in him, which is the head of all principality and power.*

In whom alfo ye are circumcifed with the circumcifion made without hands, in putting off the body of the fins of the flefh, by the circumcifion of Chrift:

Buried with him in baptifm, wherein alfo you are rifen with him through the faith of the operation of God, who hath raifed him from the dead.

The 5, 6, 7, and 8. Verfes of that aforementioned *Rom.* 6. are Exegetical of the two aforefaid Texts, *Rom.* 6. 4. and *Col.* 2. 12. and do clearly unfold and demonftrate the Apoftles meaning of Believers, Elect Perfons, being buried with Chrift

Chrift in Baptifm, which I take to be this chiefly, *viz*. When our Saviour Chrift was Crucified, Dead and Buried, all the fins of Gods Elect, young and old, from *Adam* to the very laft Soul, that fhall be faved, lay upon him, *Ifa*. 53. and were crucified, flain, and buried in the Grave with him: For when Chrifts Body, that Holy Temple, was deftroyed, the Body of Sin alfo was deftroyed, but that Temple was Raifed up again, and built in three Days, as the Lord faid, but the Body of Sin remained in the Grave, and Death for ever holds that, but it could not hold our Saviour; and the Lives of all the Elect of God being hid in Chrift from all Eternity, did vertually rife with him at his Refurrection, and then he was juftified, and fully acquitted from all the fins of Gods Elect, having made plenary fatisfaction to the Juftice of God, and fulfilled all Righteoufnefs, all the Elect of God were juftified in him decretally, *Eph*. 2. 6, 7.

Rom. 8.-*Who fhall lay any thing to the charge of Gods elect? It is God that juftifieth: Who is he that condemneth? It is Chrift that died, yea rather that is rifen again, who is even at the right hand of God, who alfo maketh interceffion for us.* For my part, I muft confefs, I cannot fee which way they can Dip any thing out of thefe Scriptures, to give any Authority for Dipping the whole Bodies of Men and Women under Water in Baptifm; for if there be any pofitive Command for it, or any Example in it, as they require of us for Infant-Baptifm, it lies fo deep that it cannot be drawn up.

But there is that in it which gives Light and Countenance to Infants Baptifm, by the Apoftles joining Spiritual Circumcifion the Type, with Spiritual Baptifm the Antitype, and Circumcifion is

placed

placed firſt in order of time: For as Circumciſion was firſt adminiſtred to Adult Perſons, in the firſt Inſtitution of that Ordinance, which did Initiate the Parents into the Covenant, then for ever after it belonged only to the Jews Children, who were to be circumciſed or deſtroyed in their Childhood, *Exod.* 17. 14. And to Adult, proſylited Gentiles, and their young Children alſo, at eight Days old: Their Children were not to ſtay for the Ordinance of Circumciſion until they came to Years of Diſcretion, to be capable to make a profeſſion of their Faith perſonally.

Even ſo Baptiſm, at its firſt Inſtitution, was firſt adminiſtred to Adult Believers, and then to their Children; as in the caſe of the Jaylor, and ſeveral other whole Houſholds, that occaſionally are mentioned, as ſome particular Perſons are on the ſame Score, though no doubt to be made, but that there were Thouſands of whole Houſes, as well as theſe the Apoſtle mentions, that were baptized in the Apoſtles time, at the firſt Plantation of the Goſpel Churches; ſo that Baptiſm did ſucceed and ſupply the office or uſe of Circumciſion, and maketh the ſame Figure now in the Church of God, under the Goſpel, as Circumciſion did in the Church of God under the Law; therefore all the Children of believing Parents ought to be baptized, notwithſtanding Mens cavilling, and carping, and forbidding of it.

2. In *Page* 3. this Authour queries whether I would make a new Bible, becauſe I aſſerted, that Elect dying Infants are ſaved by Habitual Faith; for it is the Salvation of ſuch that I treated about in all my Book, at which he ſcoffingly replyed, that I am pleaſed with an unſcriptural Baptiſm, and that I adventured to prove it in ſuch a way,

and

and by such Topicks and Mediums, that both the Universities could hardly ever think of.

'And faith he, that Children are saved by
'Christ, we have asserted, because we know of
'no other name but Jesus; but that they are sa-
'ved by Faith, Habitual Faith in Christ, I must
'confess, I never read it in all the Book of God.
'I wish he could shew me the *Chapter* where
'Christ said any such thing, that Infants are sa-
'ved by Habitual Faith.

1. Pray look into that *Chapter* where you find that God hath declared two ways for the saving Elect Persons, one for the saving of dying Infants without the Grace of Faith, and the other for saving Adult Believers by Faith, and in the very next *Verse* after you shall find Habitual Faith: Shew me but where the one is, and I will quickly shew you where the other is; and if you miss of it there, then

2. Look into that Scripture where you find that Christ hath said, in so many Words, that none shall have the Grace of Faith, or are capable of receiving of it, but Adult Persons, and next unto it you will find Habitual Faith for Elect dying Infants.

3. If you fail of finding it there, then look into *Gen.* 17. 7. and if you can find the Covenant of Peculiarity made to *Abraham*, which you say is dissolved, and I am sure in the very next Verse after you will find Habitual Faith for the Salvation of Elect dying Infants: But however put on your Spectacles, and behold that 1 *John* 3. 9. and there you may find Habitual Faith, that you pretend you are so much a Stranger unto, though not in so many Words, yet in that which is equivalent, in these Words, *Whosoever is born of God, doth not commit sin; for his seed remain-*

eth

eth in him: and he cannot sin, because he is born of God.

Pray what is this Seed of God? Is it not Habitual Grace? And can there be Habitual Grace, and not the Grace of Faith? Whereas Faith is set for all the Graces of the Spirit frequently in Scripture. Here you see all that are born of God have this Habit or Seeds of God, remaining in them, and God will save none, either old or young, but such as are Regenerated, and born again; therefore dying Infants must have Habitual Grace, or they can never be saved.

Now, Sir, you shall see that I will bring in Mr. *Hercules* to witness against Mr. *Collins*, in Page 6. where you quote Mr. *Charnock*, in favour of your Opinion, and so make his Words your own, in these Words, ' As Christ had a Body prepared ' him to do the Work of a Mediator, so the Soul ' hath a Habit prepared to do the Work of the ' new Creature; as the corrupt Nature is the ' Habit of Sin, so the new Nature is the Habit of ' Grace: God doth not only call us to believe, ' love, and obey, but brings in the Grace of Faith, ' Love, and Obedience. This Habit receives various ' Denominations.

Now could it ever have been thought, that this Man should make himself such a Stranger to the very notion of Habitual Faith? I would fain know of this Authour, what difference there is between Habitual Grace, and Habitual Faith; for I have always taken Faith to be Grace, ever since I have been acquainted with the Grace of God; therefore faith is no Grace, or this Man is miserably mistaken, and out of the way: But we find faith set down alone for all the Graces of the Spirit, frequently in the Holy Scripture; for he owns Habitual Grace, and derides Habitual Faith.

Thus

Thus he is a Witness against himself; for what any Man quotes, though of another Mans words, to justify his own Principle or Opinion by, they are in a sense, as much his own, as if they came originally from himself.

Sir, you say in Page 4. that I had given away the Cause and Habitual Faith too; but if I did, you have been extraordinary kind unto me; for you have given me my Cause again, and your own to boot. But,

2. As for the Jaylor, we do not read, that any one of his Houshold believed before they were baptized but himself, nor that any of them did exercise the Grace of faith, but the Jaylor himself; yet the next Verse tells us, that he believed in God with all his House. Now what will you call that Faith which they had? We do not find that it was Actual, then it must be Habitual, and they were Habitual Believers; for the Habit and Seeds of Gods Grace was just newly planted in them, it was not above an Hours time between the Jaylors Conversion and Baptism; therefore the Grace they had then, at that time, had but little time to grow and exert it self in him, who was Adult; but we find no Grace acted by any of the rest.

Again say you, as if it came from Mr. *Charnock*,

'Hence habits are as Seeds, which makes the
'Earth capable to bring forth good fruit; but
'what good fruit hath an Infant with all his Ha-
'bitual Grace?

'Now let all these Characters of Habitual Grace
'be put together, and then consider whether any
'of these things can affect little Infants. I hope
'by this time you have enough of Habitual
'Faith.

How dare you deal so disingenuously by Mr. *Charnock*,

Charnock, to make an Anabaptist of him now he is dead, (for he was none when he was living,) by enveloping your own Sentiments and Notions with his, as if it came from him, without any distinction in your quotation. This might pass for a popish Miracle.

4. I must confess, if Adult Persons, by the strength and power of Humane Wisdom and Carnal Reason, can acquire Grace, and are the Authors and Finishers of their own Faith and Eternal Salvation, then these things cannot affect little Infants.

But forasmuch as the Creature is wholly passive in the Reception of Grace, and Christ is all in all from the foundation of Mans Salvation to the Top-stone thereof, therefore a young Child in the Womb, or in the Cradle, is as capable of being born again, as the oldest Sinner upon Earth, and Christ can raise a young Sinner from the dead, as well as an old one, for both old and young are dead in Trespasses and Sins, before they are converted, and the Grace of God take hold of them, and raise them from the Dead; and a Child would as soon come to Christ of himself, as an old Man, for they both lie dead in Trespasses and Sins; and the Apostle saith, *And you hath he quickened who were dead in trespasses and sins.*

5. Let any Impartial Man strictly observe, and he shall find, that the whole Strength and Bent of this Authours Arguments against Infants Baptism do as naturally tend to the making Adult Believers the Authors of their own Faith, and Eternal Salvation, as it is for the Sparks to fly upwards. The Scripture saith, *By grace are ye saved through faith, and that not of your selves, it is the gift of God.*

May

May not an Elect dying Child in the Cradle have Habits in him, infused by the blessed Spirit of Grace, as well as the living Child in the womb, have the Habits of Reason and Understanding planted in him by the same Hand, though he cannot exercise his Reason and Understanding? O for shame cease from bringing your carnal Reason and humane Wisdom into the Ballance, against the free Grace of God; consider what the Apostle saith, 1 Cor. 2. *But God hath chosen the foolish things of the world to confound the wise, and God hath chosen the weak things of the world to confound the things that are mighty. And base things of the world, and things which are despised, hath God chosen, yea, and things which are not, to bring to nought things that are.* And who are weaker than Children? And yet the Scripture saith, Psal. 8. *Out of the mouth of babes and sucklings hast thou ordained strength,* &c. Our Saviour said, *Have ye never read, out of the mouth of babes and sucklings thou hast perfected praise.* And who are more despised by you than Children are, in that common saying of yours, *What are young Children capable of?* Here you may see our Saviour Christ tells ye what they are capable of; and Gods design in this, is That no Flesh should glory in his presence.

Luther saith in his Book, Page 122, 123, 'If 'Circumcision was valued upon the account of 'the Promise, and the Promise cannot be recei-
'ved but by Faith, then this follows, that little 'Children, by the co-operation of the Holy Spi-
'rit, may have Faith, and the Heart of an Adult 'Person is no more capable of changing himself 'than an Infant.

Another saith, 'That a Man is as truly bound 'to lay hold of the Promise, and cast himself up-
'on it for his Children, as for himself.

Mr.

Mr. *Marſhal* in Page 78. faith, ' Farther to the
' Glory of the Grace of God, that this union is
' fully accompliſhed by Chriſt giving the Spirit
' of Faith to us, even before we can act Faith in
' the Reception of him; becauſe by this Grace,
' or Spirit of faith, the Soul is inclined to an
' active receiving of Chriſt, and no doubt, Chriſt
' thus united to many Infants, which have the
' Spirit of Faith, becauſe they are not come to
' the Years of underſtanding.

Where are you now with your humane, invented, lame, decrepit Salvation? What! do you think it will paſs becauſe you have cafed it over, as Men do falſe Money, with that bleſſed Term, the Imputation of Chriſts Righteouſneſs, without the uniting Grace of Faith; for where there is no Faith there is no other Grace: So that inſtead of ſaving Elect dying Infants by Grace through Faith, and that not of their ſelves, you tacitely ſay, they are ſaved without Grace, and that not of faith, but by a new-found way; this is to pervert the Scripture with a witneſs: You ſay dying Infants may be ſaved, and yet are not capable of receiving the Grace of faith, and the Holy Ghoſt faith, that without faith it is impoſſible to pleaſe God; now who ſhall we believe, the Holy Ghoſt that contradicts you, or you that contradict the Holy Ghoſt, let the Reader judge, and give it on your ſide if he can.

To conclude this Head, Sir, You do allow, That all Adult Believers are ſaved through faith in the Imputation of Chriſts Righteouſneſs and Merits, and no other way: I know you do allow this, wherefore I do boldly challenge you in the name of the Lord, to produce but one Text of Scripture, throughout the whole Book of God, that doth diſcover any other way or means, wherein in God hath ordained and appointed to save Elect dying Infants in, differing in any point, or part of it, from that wherein he saves Adult Believers.

But if you cannot, then who hath made a new Bible, you or I? For I am sure, there is no such way in the old one; therefore never value your self more upon this new-found, fictitious way: But of this more hereafter, when I come to treat about the many ways that one of your Brethren hath asserted there are for the saving Elect dying Infants, which (saith he) we know not of. One that read your Book made this Remark,

(Saith he) 'Pages 4 and 5 are spent in pro-
' ving, that Infants are saved by Christs Righte-
' ousness without Faith, and grown Persons by
' Faith in the same Righteousness: *Query*, Whe-
' ther there be two ways of Salvation? If there
' be, where is it explained, in the Scripture?
' I do not mean a new one of Mans making.

3. Now, Sir, for a farther Answer to your scoffing, deriding, and ridiculing Infants Habitual Faith, in that Page aforesaid, *viz.* 6.

1. I begin thus, That all the Seed of believing Parents are in the Everlasting Covenant, which God made with *Abraham*, is most evident, because they were never cast out, as I shall clearly prove hereafter, though here is a Text that is sufficient to prove it, *Gal.* 3. 17, 18. *And this I say, that the covenant that was confirmed before of God in Christ, the Law which was four hundred and thirty years after, cannot disanul, that it should make the promise of none effect.*

For if the inheritance be of the Law, it is no more of promise: but God gave it to Abraham by promise. And cast your Eye back upon the 14*th*.

B   2. All

2. All the Seed of Believers under the Gospel tio partake of all the Benefits and Priviledges of that Covenant, as much as ever the Seed of professing Jews did under the Law, if not more, unless it be those whose Parents, by their Cruelty unto them, deprive them of it:

And therefore they have as good a Right to the Ordinance of the Initiating Seal, or Token of the Covenant, namely Baptism, as ever the Jews Children had to the Token, or Initiating Seal of the Covenant, under the Law, namely, the Ordinance of Circumcision.

3. That it is so, doth clearly appear from our Saviour Christ's Carriage and Deportment towards those little Children, that were brought unto him.

1. Let us consider whose Children they were, which were brought unto him.

2. Who they were, that brought them.

3. Who they were, that rebuked them which brought them.

4. What were they brought unto Christ for.

5. And Lastly, What profit or benefit did they receive from Christ.

1. These Children, that were brought unto him, were the Children of Believers.

2. They which brought them were such as believed in him; for had they been Enemies, they would never have brought their Children unto him, in expectation of receiving a blessing from him.

3. Those that rebuked them, which brought them unto him, were his own Disciples, *Mark* 10. 13. *And they brought young children to him, that he should touch them ; and his disciples rebuked those that brought them.*

Verse

Verse 14. *But when Jesus saw it, he was much displeased, and said unto them, Suffer the little children to come unto me, and forbid them not: for of such is the kingdom of God;* that is, the Church.

4. They were brought unto Christ to be blessed by him, and that he should pray over them, *Mat.* 19. 13.

5. And Lastly, They did not lose their Expectation, for they were blessed by him, *Mark* 10. 16. *And he took them up in his arms, put his hands upon them, and blessed them.* —

Christ did bless them with spiritual Blessings, for it was that they were brought unto him for; because we do not find, they had any bodily Diseases, or Infirmities to be cured of: And as for Temporal Blessings, though Christ, as God, was Lord Proprietor of all the World, yet as he was Man, he was poorer than the Fowls of the Air, or the Foxes of the Earth; therefore they did not come unto him for Temporal Blessings, but Spiritual: They were brought unto him, that he would lay his hands on them, and pray: Christ liked their Arrand they came on, or else he would not have been displeased with those that rebuked them: And Christ did pray for them, and laid his hands on them, and blessed them; and Christ pray'd for none, but for the Elect, which he died for, *John* 17. 9. *I pray for them: I pray not for the world, but for them which thou hast given me, for they are thine.*

Therefore these little Children were in Christ, and Members of his Mystical Body, the Church. But it may be objected, Christ did not baptize them, nor command that they should be baptized. 1. Christ himself baptized none. 2. As they were the Children of believing Parents, no doubt but they were baptized before they were

brought

brought to Christ, or else without all peradventure, Christ would have given command to baptize them; for I think, none will be so bold as to deny that they had a Right to the Ordinance of Baptism, when it is declared, that Christ blessed them, who should have forbid Water, that they should not have been baptized, as well as the rest of Christs Disciples, who had received the Graces of the Spirit, as well as they: And if they had been baptized afterwards, it would have been upon Record in the Holy Scriptures, as well as all the Circumstances are, that did attend his Blessing of them; therefore I do conclude, that all the Children of believing Parents were baptized in their Infancy, in the first Plantation of the Gospel Church Dispensation.

For as soon as Adult Heathens were converted and baptized, if they had any Children they were all baptized with them, as being parts of themselves as the Jaylor and his Houshold were; for the Children are taken into Covenant with their Parents when they themselves are.

2. That *Timothy* was baptized when he was a Child, me-thinks it ought not to be doubted; for, (1.) his Grandmother *Lois* was an eminent Christian: (2.) His Mother *Eunice* was a zealous godly Woman: And, (3.) He himself was a Believer from his Childhood; but we never read of his being baptized, when he was Adult; yet of his circumcision we do, but that he was baptized, either in his Childhood, or at his riper years, is beyond all peradventure; because if he had not been baptized, he could not have been a Bishop; for no Person is, or ought to be received into a Church, as a private Member thereof, unless they are baptized; much less a Church Officer, of that Magnitude as *Timothy* was; therefore

fore he was baptized in his Childhood, as being the Son of a Holy Mother.

3. That there have been Infant believing Church-Members in Gospel-times, is a great Truth; and therefore all the Children of believing Parents are Church-Members still. Pray read and consider that in *Matth.* 18. 1, 2, 3, 4, 5, 6. for it is very apposite to our purpose, notwithstanding our Authour's scoffing, and deriding of it, in Pages 5, 6.

1 *At the same time came the disciples unto Jesus, saying, Who is the greatest in the kingdom of heaven?*

2 *And Jesus called a little child unto him, and set him in the midst of them,*

3 *And said, Verily I say unto you, Except ye be converted, and become as little children, ye shall not enter into the kingdom of heaven.*

5 *And whoso shall receive one such little child in my name, receiveth me.*

Mr. *Cotton* said, 'That the laying Christ's 'hands on these little Children, that were 'brought unto him, was to adopt them into 'the Family of *Israel*, as *Jacob* did the two 'Sons of *Joseph* into his Family, which was the 'Church of God.

But to observe Christ's words to his Disciples;
1. Here is something to be observed from this distinction that Christ did make of this Child from the common sort of Children, in that he said, *Whoso shall receive one such little child in my name*, &c.

For if it had been spoken of Children in the general, then it would have been said, Whoso receives any Child, and not any such little Child; and what sort of little Child this was, the next Verse

Verse tells us; for he was one of them which believed in Christ:

Ver. 6. *But whoso shall offend one of these little ones which believe in me, it were better for him that a milstone were hanged about his neck, and he were drowned in the depth of the sea.*

Let them have a care that offend and hinder them from coming to Christ, in the Ordinance of Baptism, for I know of no other visible way there is for young Infants to come, or be brought unto Christ in, but that.

But for a farther opening, and explaining these words;

1. Let us consider the occasion of this Speech of our Saviour's to his Disciples.

2. What part of these words did relate to the old Disciples.

3. What part of them did belong to the Infant Disciples.

4. And Lastly, What our Saviours design was in all this.

1. As for the occasion of the words it was thus, The Disciples asked Christ, Who is greatest, not who should be greatest in the Kingdom of Heaven; which Kingdom of Heaven, was either the Church Militant, or the Church Triumphant in Glory, or both: But I am inclinable to believe, this was spoken of the Church on Earth, because the Disciples had been disputing among themselves, who should be greatest; and therefore they came to our Saviour to decide the difference by that Question aforesaid, *Who is greatest in the kingdom of heaven?*

2. These words were spoken principally to the old Disciples; for our Saviour Christ perceived a Spirit of Pride and Ambition crawling into them;

for they had a mind to know of Chrift, who of them he efteemed to be the greateſt among them in the Church; therefore our Bleſſed Redeemer called for one of theſe little Children, which believed on him, and fet him in the midſt of them, and then he made a Speech unto the Adult Believers, to humble them, and alſo to inform our Judgments, and to be a Caution unto all Chriſtians in future Ages.

1. It was to humble the Difciples, to let them know, that it was not their Maturity of Years, or Humane Difcretion, that was the neceſſary Qualification for the Reception of Grace; but as if our Saviour ſhould have ſaid, Do you ſee this little Child, in whom I have poured my Spirit of Grace: Why there was no more in one of you to recommend the Grace of God unto you, than there was in this little Child; but more to oppoſe and hinder the work of God upon ye; for this little Child had nothing but Original Sin to hinder, but you had both Original and Actual Sins alſo to oppoſe it.

2. As if Chriſt ſhould have ſaid, You were as paſſive in the reception of my Grace, as this little Child was, and you ſee that he is humble, he is not ſeeking to be great, nor ambitious of worldly Honour: Do you learn of this little Child; be not high-minded, nor ſtrive to be great; but be you humble; for you have no more to be proud of, than this little Child hath.

3. It may be objected, How could this be ſpoken to the Difciples? for they were converted ſome time before this was ſpoken; but theſe Perſons to whom Chriſt ſpake theſe words, were to be converted, and become as that little Child.

1. To this I Anſwer, (It is true,) Chriſts Difciples were converted before, all but *Judas*, who never

never was to be converted, becaufe he was a Son of Perdition; and *Peter* was converted long before our Saviour faid unto him, *When thou art converted ſtrengthen thy Brethren.*

• 2. There are Converfions to be wrought after the firft Converfion, in which the Sinner is turned from darknefs to Light, from a ftate of fin and unbelief, into a ftate of Grace; but as for the ftate of Grace, there is no need of any farther converfion as to that, for once in Chrift, and for ever in Chrift; all the Devils in Hell can never get ye out thence again; for a ftate of Grace is perfect, intire, lacking nothing; and of that ftate we have not the keeping, but it is fixed in the Hands of Jefus Chrift, fecure enough; for they can never fin themfelves out of that ftate again, (*Pſal.* 89. 30. to 36.) that ftate is unchangeable.

But notwithftanding this, there is need of daily Converfions to be wrought, for and in Believers, becaufe they fin daily; wherefore Chrift hath commanded Believers to watch againft Sin and Temptations, and pray daily for pardoning Mercy, to befeech God to keep them from Temptation, to forgive and abfolve all their fins in the Blood of Chrift; and this doth more efpecially concern Believers, than Sinners; for none can call God Father, but by the Spirit of Chrift, that dwelleth in them.

3. The moft holieft Saint upon Earth, finneth daily; for *in many things we offend all*, faith the Apoftle, and in *Eccl.* 7. 20. *For there is not a juſt man upon earth that doeth good, and finneth not.*

1 John 1. 8, 9, 10. *If we ſay that we have no ſin, we deceive our ſelves, and the truth is not in us.*

If we confeſs our ſins, he is faithful, and juſt to forgive us our ſins, and to cleanſe us from all unrighteouſneſs.   If

If we say that we have not sinned, we make him a liar, and his word is not in us.

Here are three things to be noted from these Scriptures, 1. It is a very dangerous thing to say we have no sin, for we deceive our selves, which is the greatest deceit of all. 2. If we confess our sins, God is both merciful and just, and therefore he will pardon, if we confess our sins in prayer unto him. 3. And Lastly, If we say that we have not sinned, we are guilty of Blasphemy, because thereby we make God a Liar by contradiction. That all Believers do sin daily is an undeniable Truth : I will appeal to any Believers Conscience, for Judgment of this; and also, that daily watchfulness against sin, and prayer to God for pardon of sin is the Believers Duty during life.

4. A Spiritual state is not a sufficient Guard to secure the Believer in a spiritual frame of heart, though it secures him from falling totally from Grace, yet it cannot secure him from falling into sin ; it must be fresh supplies of Grace that must do that.

5. That this was spoken in favour of little Children, which believed in Christ, is very clear,

For Jesus called a little Child unto him, and set [him] in the midst of [them]: (1.) Here is [him] the young Disciple, and (2.) [them] the old Disciples : (3.) Here Christ takes his Observation from the believing young Disciple ; And (4.) He makes his Application to the Adult Disciples : (5.) Christ commended the little Disciples Humility ; And (6.) He reprehended the grown Disciples, for their Pride and Ambition : (7.) And lastly, Our Saviour Christ, for a farther demonstration of his peculiar Love and Grace to these Infant Believers, hath denounced a most a most dreadful Threatning against any Person that shall offend them; and I know none that offend them more among Christians than they do, that hinder them from being brought unto Christ in the Ordinance of Baptism.

6. The Gracious End of Christ in all this was, (1.) To humble his old Disciples: (2.) For a Caution unto all succeeding Generations: (3.) And lastly, To let us all know, that the Glory of Gods Free Grace doth shine forth as conspicuous in the Salvation of Elect Babes, as it doth in the Salvation of an old Sinner; for both are in a like condition by nature, when the Spirit of God comes to work first upon them; for the young Child is spiritually dead in the first *Adam*, and so is the old Sinner also; therefore the Spirit of God raiseth one as soon, and as easie, as the other; for both are passive, and have no hand at all in their own Conversion, no more than a Child hath in bringing himself into the World, or than *Lazarus* had in raising himself from the dead: *Eph.* 2. 1. *And you hath he quickned, who were dead in trespasses and sins.*

7. And Lastly, Christ saith, *Suffer little children, and forbid them not to come unto me, for of such is the kingdom of God:* This is the Church of which all the Seed of Believers are Members as much now, as ever the Jews Children were under the Law, as I shall clearly prove before I have done with you; for it is the very same Church State, though in another Dress, or under another dispensation. Our Saviour Christ did not destroy the Church State, when he excommunicated them unbelieving Jews, and received in the Gentiles, no more than we do, when we excommunicate Persons and take in Members into the Church: And here you may see this proved from our Saviour's

threatning

threatning the Jews, *Mat.* 21. *The kingdom of God shall be taken from you, and given to a nation bringing forth the fruit thereof.* God did Excommunicate many Thousands of the unbelieving Jews, and their Posterity, and took the Gentiles, and their Seed, into the Church; and of such is the Kingdom of God. Christ took away the Kingdom of God from the Jews, and gave it unto the Gentiles; and there is the same Subjects in the Kingdom of God now, as there was then, namely, Believers and their Children, *Acts* 2. 39. And these Infant Church-Members are under the Care, Tuition, and Ministry of the Holy and Blessed Angels, *Mat.* 18. 10. Heb. 1. 14. *Are they not all ministring spirits, sent forth to minister for them who shall be the heirs of salvation?*

Now consider all these things rightly, and it will appear infallibly, that the Children of believing Parents are Church-Members, and as such, have an Indubitable Right unto the Ordinance of Baptism; in which Ordinance all the Subjects baptized are passive: Our Saviour Christ himself was passive, and the Eunuch was passive, in their Baptism; for they were not a baptizing as they travelled along the way to the Water, nor as they came from the Water, (as our Authour dreams in Page 9.) but they were baptized when the Water was applied to their Flesh, and not before. Our Saviour Christ nor the Eunuch, did not apply the Water themselves to themselves in Baptism, therefore they were passive, and so were all those that were circumcised; and therefore Baptism came in the room of Circumcision; for there is no other Ordinance, but these two in the Church, in which Persons were to be passive; therefore the one makes the same passive Figure

in

in the Church now, as the other did in the Church then: And that our Saviour Chrift was paffive in his Baptifm, appeareth clearly by what paft between him and *John* the Baptift. This was that which made *John* the Baptift ſō loath to baptize our Saviour Chrift; for he thought it would be a degradation unto his Holy Majefty, for him to be active, and his Lord and Mafter paffive; but our Saviour Chrift faid, *Suffer it to be so now*, Mat. 3. 13, 14, 15.

But, faith our Authour, Chrift did it as an Act of Righteoufnefs, and therefore he was not paffive in his Baptifm; and fo was Chrift's coming into the World, and dying for Sinners, an Act of Righteoufnefs; becaufe in that he fulfilled all Righteoufnefs for all the Elect, which he had ingaged to do from all Eternity; and his Water-Baptifm in which he was paffive, was but a Figure, which reprefented his bloody Baptifm, in which he was alfo paffive, *Luke* 1. *But I have a baptifm to be baptized with, and how am I ſtraitned till it be accomplifhed*: That was his crucifiction, which he there called his Baptifm. I fuppofe none will fay, that our Saviour Chrift was active in his fufferings, though he was active to his fufferings; and fo he was active to his Baptifm alfo; but he was paffive [in] both.

Therefore that all Perfons, young and old, are paffive in Baptifm, is an unfhaken Truth; wherefore this Argument of our Authours may take place among the reft of his lame ones, which are but [all] in his Book. Thus you fee who thefe little Children were, that our Saviour Chrift fpake thefe Things of: They were Believers, and not Adult Difciples.

For had our Saviour Chrift been fpeaking or treating with his Enemies about Adult Difciples,
then.

then indeed it might have been spoken of them, and not to them, as the Frame of our Saviour's Speech was bent with a refpect to thofe Children, as in fome places of Scripture we find the fame Epithet given to Adult Believers; but then there is that which doth accompany it, that makes it clearly appear to be fo; but here is nothing at all, neither in this bleffed caution, nor in this fweet Reprehenfion of our Saviour Chrift's to his Difciples, that does any way make it appear to be fo.

For here were no other Subjects concerned in this Speech of our Saviour Chrift's in *Matt.* 18. but two forts of Perfons, namely, old Difciples, and young: Therefore that all the Children of believing Parents are Church-Members, and do continue to be fo, unlefs they do cut themfelves off, by their own Unbelief and Unfruitfulnefs, their Parents, by cutting themfelves off as the Jews did, *John* 15. *Every branch in me that beareth not fruit, is taken away.* The Jews unchurched themfelves, who were the natural Seed of *Abraham*, to whom the Covenant, as to them, was firft made, *Rom.* 11. But the Covenant was not diffolved, nor the Church-State deftroyed. This is a great Truth, notwithftanding all the Cavils and Quibbles of the Adverfaries; and this their fcoffing Argument may be fent to the Hofpital among the reft of their fick and decrepit Ones, to be cured.

4. In Page 2. faith this Authour, *Rev.* 20. 12. *cannot affect little Infants, which have no works, good nor bad*; *therefore it cannot be here intended of fuch.*

To this I anfwer thus. That although little Infants have no perfonal Works of their own, good

nor

nor bad, in an ordinary way, yet relatively considered they have : Now to diftinguifh in this nice point, as the Lord fhall inable me.

1. In *Adam* we are all polluted, our very Natures contaminated, and our Blood tainted; our firft Parents being found guilty, and condemned for Spiritual High Treafon, againft the King of Kings; and fo a little Child in the Womb, or in the Cradle, is as much polluted and depraved; as the oldeft Sinner upon Earth, and not onely fo, but the very Act of our firft Parents Rebellion becomes theirs alfo, by Imputation; for *Adam*'s very Act of Unbelief and Difobedience is as much theirs, as ever it was his own; for we are all included in Unbelief, young Infants, as well as old Sinners, all have finned, and come fhort of the Glory of God; fo that *Adam*'s firft Act of fin comes to be theirs by Imputation, as much every whit, as if they had tranfacted it in their own Perfons. And thus you fee, that although little Children have no perfonal bad Works, yet they have relative bad Works, which comes to be their own by Tranfmiffion, from the Loyns of the firft *Adam*, who was the natural common Head, and Reprefentative of all Man-kind.

2. But on the other hand, Although Elect dying Infants have no perfonal good Works of their own, yet they have relative good Works, which are more their own, as to benefit, then if they had perfonally done them themfelves; for they are meritorious works, and that no meer Mans can be, though never fo great a Saint: So that in that fenfe, they are more their own, than if they had, or poffibly could have perfonally performed them of themfelves; and thefe are the Works, which Chrift the Second *Adam* hath brought forth for them, and that perfonally too

upon

upon the Cross, who is the Head, and Representative of all the Elect of God.

For as in the first *Adam* all died, even so in Christ, the second *Adam*, shall all be made alive, *Rom.* 5. *Therefore as by the offence of one judgment came upon all men to condemnation: even so by the righteousness of one, the free gift came upon all men unto justification of life.*

For as by one mans disobedience many were made sinners: so by the obedience of one, shall many be made righteous.

As the first *Adam's* unbelief and disobedience was the Elect dying Infants, by Imputation, as well as Adult Persons, *viz.* Believers:

Even so the Righteousness and Obedience of Christ, are made theirs by Imputation, through the Grace of Faith; for Faith is not onely the Gift of God, but also the work of God; for it is God gives it unto them, and also works it in them all, both young and old, that doth belong to the Election of Grace, *Heb.* 12. 2. *Isa.* 26. 12. *Phil.* 2. 13.

God is a free Agent, and he bestows his Grace when he please, where he please, and works how he please, and in whom he please, both on old or young.

And Christ's Obedience, which was as well active as passive, personal and perfect, is all as much an Elect dying Infant's from the Womb, or the Cradle, as ever it was the oldest Saints upon Earth, or in Heaven either; for Christ is the Authour of Eternal Salvation, as well as of Faith, and the Finisher of both, *Eph.* 2. *Heb.* 12.

Therefore young Children, as well as Adult Persons, must all stand before the Lord, in the Day of Judgment, and be Judged, determined,

and

and receive Eternal Sentence, according to their Works, together with Adult Persons.

Wherefore if this Text, in *v.* 20. 12. doth not affect little Infants, as our Authour affirms, he ought to have produced one more to the purpose, and not to leave us in the Dark, in this Point.

5. Saith our Authour in Page 5. *We do affirm, that Infants may be fit for the Kingdom of God, as our Lord hath said, and yet not qualified for Gospel Ordinances.* To this I Answer,

Our Saviour Christ saith, *Except a man be born again, he cannot see, nor enter into the kingdom of God*, *John* 3. 3, 5. And no Children can be fit for the Kingdom of God, until they are regenerated and born again, and then they have the Grace of Faith planted in them, which can never be plucked up again; for the new Creature must have all its Members, it must have Faith, or it cannot see the Kingdom of God; for Faith is the Eyes of the new Creature, and there is no Person that is born again, but hath the Grace of Faith; for were it possible, for any Soul to be born again without it, that Soul would be born blind, and could never see his way to Heaven, nor enter into it.

The new Creature in a Child, either in the Womb, or in the Cradle, is as perfect and compleat, in all its Lineaments, as it is in the oldest Saint upon Earth; therefore the new Creature, though but in a Child, can see as far as the new Creature can in the oldest Believer on Earth, and is as capable of transforming Views of Jesus Christ: And we are not altogether without a Precedent of this kind, in the case of *John* the Baptist, in the very Womb, *Luke* 1. 44. And if

the

the Children of believing Parents are capable of receiving the Grace of Faith, who should forbid Water, that they should not be baptized? For no Children can be fit for the Kingdom of Heaven, without Faith; for without Faith it is impossible to please God, and God will save none but such as he is well pleased with, and reconciled unto; therefore this Argument must be sent to the rest also.

Lastly, I observe that this Authour doth Reflect much upon the Ignorance of little Children; he seems to make the Ignorance of young Infants to be too hard a Match for the Wisdom and Power of God, and renders Infants wholly incapable of receiving the Seeds and Habits of his Grace, and thereby he doth make the Infusion of Grace, to stand in the Wisdom of Men at Years of Discretion, which reflects great dishonour upon all the Glorious Attributes of God.

But pray, Sir, (now I think on't) produce us but one plain Text of Scripture, to prove where our Lord hath said any such thing, as that Children may be fit for the Kingdom of God, and not for Gospel Ordinances, (but it is the Ordinance of Baptism that you mean,): or must we believe it, because you say it is so? Your own Party may do it, if they please, but I will not, for my part.

Now, Sir, I will not say you are in a Noose, as you have said of me in Page 14. which is a Term of Art, better becoming the Office of a *Tyburn* Executioner, than the Office of a Gospel Minister: But however, this I will say, You are sufficiently entangled, get out as well as you can.

6. In

6. In Page 7. you have charged me falfly, and upon that falfe charge, you raifed an Argument againſt me, which is ſuitable to all the reſt of your lame foundered Jades.

For ſay you, *Thoſe Children of Believers, which die in an unregenerate ſtate, either never had the Habits of Grace, or elſe if they had them, they have loſt them; but there is no loſing Habits of Grace, Ergo, they never had them: If you ſay they had them, and have loſt them, that is againſt your own Principle about Perſeverance: If you ſay they never had them, then you contradict your own Book, which Aſſerts, that all the Infants of Believers have it; and therefore you baptize them: Get out of this Priſon as well as you can.*

Pray Friend take notice, that it is Five Pound an Hour for falſe Impriſonment.

This Gentleman doth juſt as little Boys do, that make a Thing of Rags, in imitation of a Cock, and when they have made him, then they ſet him up, and ſtand at a diſtance, and throw at him, and when they ſtrike him down, then they rejoyce and leap, ſaying, The Cock is down, The Cock is down, when it is nothing, but a Bundle of Rags, all the while: Even ſo is the Validity of this Argument; therefore I will put it to a fair Iſſue, which ſhall be this, Produce me but any one place, in all my whole Book, where I have aſſerted this you have charged upon me, and I will turn Anabaptiſt immediately, without any delay or procraſtination, and if you cannot do this, then I ſtand falſely charged in your Book, and Habitual Faith ſtands firm, fixt, and unſhaken in mine, notwithſtanding all the Anabaptiſtical Winds and Seas that beat againſt it: for it is founded upon the Rock Chriſt Jeſus; for there can be no Acts of Grace, where there are not

Habits

Habits of Grace first: There may be Habits of Grace without Acts, but there can be no Acts without Habits, no more than a Tree can grow without a Root.

7. In Page 41. in his former Book, he maketh ‘ the Children of Infidels to have as much pri- ‘ viledge, as the Children of Christian Believers, ‘ and that they must bring forth Fruit meet for ‘ Repentance: And,
‘ Unless Children have personal Actual Faith, ‘ they are not to meddle with Gods most holy ‘ Things.

Here you may see, if God be no more merciful to Elect dying Infants, than this Man is by his Opinion, all of them would be lost, and damned for ever.

For faith he, in Page 53. of the foresaid Book,
If any bring not forth good Fruit in his own Person, the Axe being laid to the Root of the Tree, he is to be hewn down, and cast into Eternal Fire.

I think Children are excluded Heaven by these things: But I cannot pass that former strange Assertion without Examination, therefore let us hear whether or no the Scripture hath made no difference between the Children of Christian Believers, and the Children of Turks and Infidels: Hear what the Gospel Prophet saith to this new Doctrine, in *Isa.* 44. 3. *For I will pour water upon him that is thirsty, and flouds upon the dry ground: I will pour my spirit upon thy seed, and my blessing upon thine offspring.* This was predicted of the Gentiles, wherein there is a Promise unto their Children, which the Apostle declareth again, in *Acts* 2. 39. *For the promise is unto you, and to your children, and to all that are afar off, even as many as the Lord our God shall call.*

1. Pri-

1. Primarily the Promise, which God made unto *Abraham*, was made to the Jews, and their Children.

2. It was made with *Abraham* to the Gentiles, and their Seed and Offspring, which the Prophet calls the dry Ground, which were those other Sheep, Christ tells us, that were not of that Fold: They were Sheep in Election, but not in Vocation: The Fold is the Church, which did consist then chiefly of converted, believing Jews, and their Children, in Christ's time; and these Gentile Sheep were to be brought into that Fold which the Jews were of, *John* 10. 16.

3. Is there any such Promise made to the Children of Turks, that are Infidels, in all the Bible? But it is said in *Isa.* 14. The Seed of Evil-doers shall never be renowned.

4. Look into 1 *Cor.* 7. 14. *For the unbelieving husband is sanctified by the wife, and the unbelieving wife is sanctified by the husband: else were your children unclean; but now are they holy.*

This is a Federal Holiness, as well as a Matrimonial Holiness; this latter Holiness all Children have, whose Parents were lawfully Married, and they lawfully begotten, if they were not Bastards. Do we ever read of any such Character given to the Children of Turks and Infidels, in the Sacred Scriptures, as is here given the Children of either believing Husband or Wife? Doth this Man read the Bible, or the Turkish Alcoran, that doth thus boldly assert these Things? It may be in the latter, but I am sure there is no such thing in the former.

8. In Page 4. faith this Authour, *Pray give us some Scriptural Intimations, that Infants have Faith, and we will say no more.* To this I Answer,

You

You have not stated your Proposition right, it is improper, for you have fixed it in the Present Tense, for so it may as well serve for the Adult, as for Infants. How can I bring you any Scripture Intimations of this, or the other Person, that are Adult having Faith, unless we had a new Bible, made lately, while the Persons are living, with their Names in it?

But I can do more than barely produce Scripture Intimations, to prove that Children have had Faith; for they have not only had the Habit of Faith, but have also exercised it, *Luke* 1. 44. there is one; and in 2 *Tim.* 1. 5. there is another: And that there was Infant Believers, besides these, I refer to one of my former Heads, to those Children which were brought unto Christ.

9. In Page 53. of his former Book, he said, *If any bring not forth good Fruit in his own Person, the Ax being laid to the Root of the Tree, it is to be hewn down, and cast into Eternal Fire.*

Because I said he intended young and old, he is displeased: Now how can this Man pretend that he did not intend Infants by it, when it was to answer an Objection, which I shall lay down, and leave it to Judgment?

Object. 19. *Infants were once Church-Members, and that Law was never abrogated, neither do we find, they were cut off.*

If Children were not chiefly intended, as I can see no Reason to believe the contrary, by the Objection it was to Answer, yet they are wholly comprehended in that word, *If any* [without any Exception] *bring not forth good Fruit in their own Persons,* &c. For he knew that young Infants are

not

not capable of bringing forth good Fruit perſonally, in an ordinary way; therefore you did intend them, and rather than you would be at a loſs for an Anſwer to the Objection, you would doom all theſe poor Babes to Eternal Fire; but I have ſufficiently ſhewn how all Elect dying Infants do bring forth good Fruit, though not in their own Perſons, yet relatively, in the Perſon of Jeſus Chriſt, their Surety and Redeemer.

The main Theame his whole Book ran upon, both Argumentatively and Expoſtulary, was to render young Infants of believing Parents wholly uncapable of the Ordinance of Baptiſm, and Church-memberſhip; and rather than he would fail in his Enterprize, he would conſequentially condemn them all to Eternal fire: Had he left out that Word, *If any bring not forth good Fruit in their own Perſons,* &c. he might have made a ſhift to have crawl'd over it, but now he is intangled in a Snare of his own making, and let him get out if he can.

10. In Page 11. he is again troubled with the Grumbling in the Gizzard, becauſe I declared thoſe words which I met with in his former Book, which Book he values himſelf greatly upon for the bulk of it, in his pretended Anſwer to my Book; for, ſaith he, it hath 139. Pages in it: A goodly company of them! but to as little purpoſe as might be: It is more to be valued for the bulk of it, than for the Matter it contains, unleſs it be to explode their fulſome Errours.

1. I will lay down the Words that were a Prodrome to them.

2. The Words themſelves.

1. Saith he, *Let Men take heed how they put a ſlight upon the Ordinance of God, in crying up the Spirit*

:cret *design to decry the Holy Scriptures,*
wer of Godliness in Word, to undermine
dliness, &c. To this I Answer,
e Apostle *Paul* complained of those
:h had a Form of Godliness, but de-
er thereof, and commanded, that
: should turn away, 2 *Tim.* 3. 5.
ot remember, that ever I heard any
nt before; that the crying up the
dliness would undermine the form of
d if so, then the Ministers of Christ
: it in most Sermons they preach;
up the power of Godliness in every
preach, and very rarely touch up-
of Godliness; for if they have but
f Godliness, they will not be long
orm: The Apostle *Paul* no sooner
er of Godliness, but he sought out
; for he assayed to join himself to
and in the Apostles time, assoon as
converted, they were joined to the
deed there are some that cry up the
deny the Form of Godliness; But
or the power of Godliness, nor for
it all; but he was not treating about
ook, but it was with us, to answer
; but we are for the power of God-
e' Form also.
rds which I quoted were these, *They*
and Justification by Faith, to lessen Re-
holy Life.
say, you gave as a Reproof to the
: it is evident enough, that it was
t us *Pædobaptists.*
e displeased at my bearing a Testi-
t a particular Passage of a faithful
hrist, as you call him.

Wherein

Wherein (say you) *he supposed some weakness, though there was none.*

This is a very high *Encomium* indeed; What hath he no weakness in him! Then he is infallible and perfect.

2. But he doth not reckon it weakness in him, to abuse the Congregation of which, through Grace, I am an unworthy Member, in branding us with the filthy *Odium* of *Babylon*, and that we are an unbaptized Church. Pray what Name, or Character, could he have thought on to give us, that can be worse? Let any Man but see *Rev.* 17. But before I have done we shall see who is a Baptized Church, they or we.

3. Again, Is it not weakness in him to be against singing of *Psalms*? But if [he] be not guilty of weakness, that is against that Ordinance of God, then [we] are not onely guilty of weakness, but also all the Anabaptists are guilty with us, that do practice the same: And if it be not an Ordinance of God, then it is Will-worship, and all Will-worship is sin; but if it be an Ordinance of God, as from Scripture Authority it is, then it is not onely weakness in all them which oppose it, and are against it, but also wickedness, and they are in *Babylon* themselves.

4. Again, In the same Page he Reflects upon me, and calls me *Calumniator*, because that I declared in the Post-script, of my former Book, that *some of the* Anabaptists *are* Arminians, *and some gone back to* Judaism, *another sort Gormandizers on Legs of Mutton, and another sort, that are Soul-sleepers, and some of them deny the Godhead of Christ*, which latter he hath taken no notice of, neither hath he cleared them, which he did mention; and how am I a *Calumniator*, if it be true? As who dare deny it? What doth he

he think becaufe they are dipped, that that doth wafh them all clean! Or do that make Men Believers that deny the Deity of Chrift? This is a fine way of juftifying their own Principle, by juftifying tacitely fuch grofs Errors, and abominable Herefies: But as long as they are for dipping Adult Perfons, it is all well, whether they are Believers or not. O! that ever Men fhould be more for vindicating their Opinion, than of the Truths of God!

11. In Page 11. faith he, *Becaufe we withhold from Infants what Chrift would not have given them, he tells the World we make no better of Infants than Dogs.*

1. To this I anfwer, If you can fatisfie me in three things, then I will recal my Words; but if you cannot, then your Children will ftand with me, by the cruelty of your Opinion to them, no better then Dogs ftill; for if they are not in the Church, then they are out, and the Scripture faith, *Without are dogs*, Rev. 22. 15.

(1.) If you can prove by plain Scripture Teftimony, that ever Chrift, or any of his Apoftles by his Authority, did ever forbid baptizing the Infant Seed of Believers; becaufe you do pofitively declare, that you do with-hold from Infants what Chrift would not have given them, therefore you ought to have proved it by the Scripture, and not thus horribly to impofe your own uncouth Notions on the People.

(2.) You muft alfo prove from Scripture that Chrift hath any where commanded his Apoftles and Minifters to baptize none but Adult Believers, and alfo, that the Children of believing Parents muft not be baptized until they are capable of making a profeffion of their Faith:

(50)

That Scripture will not reach it in *Mat.* 28. where the Commiſſion runs, *Go and Diſciple all Nations*, &c. For Children are a part of a Nation, and the greateſt part too for number, nor will that do it in *Mark* 16. nor will that do it in *Matt.* 3. If there were no Children in *Jeruſalem*, nor in all *Judea*, nor in all the Regions round about *Jordan*, nor in all the Nations where the Goſpel is preached, or if Children be no part of Nations, then your Argument would hold Water; but otherwiſe, it is of no value at all, and ought not to be regarded.

(3.) And Laſtly, If you can produce me but one Inſtance in the Scripture, among the many Thouſands of Proſelytes, that were made and baptized, among all their Children, that was not baptized in their Infancy, but ſtayed until they came to Maturity of Years, and then made a profeſſion of their Faith, and were baptized, then I will recal it.

We read of the Elect Lady, and her Children, 2 *John* 1. 1. and of thoſe Children that believed in Chriſt, and of *Timothy*'s Mother and Grandmother, and himſelf, who were all Believers, but *Timothy* from his Childhood, whatever his Mother was, whether in her Childhood, or in her Riper Years, 2 *Tim.* 3. 15. 2 *Tim.* 1. 5. We read not a word of their being baptized, after we come to read that they believed, therefore they were baptized before, though they which were brought unto Chriſt, were then Children.

Now who dare affirm, that *Timothy* was never baptized, or that he was not baptized when he was a Child? What! not baptized, and yet a Biſhop, and ſuch an Eminent Saint, and make ſuch a Great Figure in the Church? This cannot be; for none will permit a Perſon to be a Member

to the Apostle *Paul's* Days was a long Tract of Time, and then it will appear, that those which were baptized at the first Institution might see their childrens children to be grown persons, in the Apostles time; therefore it is very strange if the Infants of Believers were not baptized in their Infancy, that we should not have so much as one single Precedent, among those many Thousands of children of believing Parents, that when he was grown up made a profession of his Faith, and was baptized; as the Proselytes to the Christian Faith were.

3. Again, Can it ever be imagined that the Jews, that were converted to the Christian Faith, would have been satisfied, if their children should not have been baptized, and be Members with them in the new Frame of Church Order and Discipline, as well as of the old one; for the Church State was the same, as I shall clearly prove hereafter, as well as the Covenant God made with *Abraham*, in which all Believers, and their Seed, are as much now, as they were under the Law.

4. If you do but consider how much the Jews stood upon their Priviledges, and in particular that of Circumcision, which belonged onely to their Eighth day Disciples, unless some Proselytes, and what stress did they lay upon it? No less than Salvation or Damnation, *Acts* 15. 1.

5. If we consider what a hard Task the Apostles had to bring them off from it, though it did belong only to their children, A̲c̲t̲s̲ 1. See there

ſtreſs they laid upon it, and ſee the
what Arguments the Apoſtles uſed
m off from it; and if they had not
ig in the room of it, that was equi-
etter, they would never have been
from it; and if it was not Baptiſm,
what it was? For my part, I know
re, agreeable than Baptiſm, becauſe
under the Law was the only Ordi-
n the Subjects were all purely paſſive,
der the Goſpel is the only Ordinance
he Subjects are purely paſſ... alſo;
were to circumciſe ... aſelves, ſo
baptize themſelves, and a child is
rform a Duty wherein the Subjects
aſſive, as an adult Perſon, and it is
to Infants than Adult Perſons, the
n of the Church or new Proſelytes
d: So that the children of believing
an undoubted Right to the Ordi-
ter Baptiſm.

Would there not have been ſome
among the Jews about it, if their
not been to be baptized? And would
been apt to ſay, [How is this?]
a Goſpel bring more Priviledge unto
of the Priviledge that our children
s is a loſing Bargain for our children;
ll the Priviledges they did enjoy unto be deſtroyed at once, by the co-
e Goſpel.

the Anabaptiſts do make very ſlight
nance of Circumciſion, and ſay it
arnal Ordinance, and no Priviledge,
very great Priviledge, for it was the
d's Everlaſting Covenant, nay it was
a Token or Mark of God's peculiar
Love

Love and Grace to that People, above all other Nations in the World: Saith the Apoftle *Rom.* 3. 1. *What advantage then hath the Jew? or what profit is there of circumcifion?*

2 *Much every way: chiefly, becaufe that unto them were committed the oracles of God.*

If you cannot fatisfie me in thefe Three Points aforefaid, I fhall not recal what I have faid concerning your children, though I hope your children will never fuffer for the Error of you their Parents.

I hope thefe Arguments, which I have already produced, are fufficient of themfelves to convince all the Anabaptifts in the World, that are not wilfully obftinate, and judicially blinded, that the baptizing of Believers children is a Gofpel Ordinance, and not a Humane Invention; and therefore it is a great Duty to perform it, and alfo a great Sin to neglect it, and it is not fuch an indifferent thing as fome Men would make it to be: But this I obferve, that thofe that thus plead are very Credules, and eafie to be impofed upon; becaufe they are Strangers, and unacquainted with their own Principles; and indeed our Author is fo kind to them, as that he himfelf doth call them Fools confequentially for their pains, in *Page* 4. Why not? For he cunningly calls all the Minifters of the Gofpel Thieves, in the middle of *Page* 10. which are for Infants Baptifm.

But me-thinks the Everlafting Covenant, which God made with *Abraham* and his Seed., fhould found in all your Ears, O! ye indifferent Ones; and never efpoufe a Principle to abufe it; for any to be for Infants Baptifm, and hold it indifferently, do but abufe it, and betray their own Principle and Ignorance into the Bargain.

Saith Mr. *Sidenham* in Page 1. 'Let this be
'considered, that there is nothing in all the New
'Testament against the baptizing of Infants, not
'one hint from any Express Word dropt from
'Christ, or his Apostles, not one Phrase which,
'though never so much strained, doth forbid such
'an Act; but there is much for it in divers Scrip-
'tures compared together, and what is wanting
'in one, is supplied in another abundantly.

12. I observe that this Authour, in his former Book, hath often quoted Mr. *Danvers*, as if he had been an infallible, spotless Authour; he ought first to have vindicated his credit and reputation, if he could, by clearing of him from those horrible, dark, and black Practices, he stands publickly charged with by Mr. *Joseph Whiston*, in his Book Intituled, *Infants Baptism from Heaven, and not of Men*: And also by Mr. *Obed Wills*, in his Book Intituled, *A Vindication of a late Treatise, Intituled, Infant Baptism Asserted and Vindicated by Scripture and Antiquity*.

1. Mr. *Whiston* in *Chap.* 1. *pag.* 1, 4, 5. Where-
'in some general Considerations Relating to the
'Authorities produced by Mr. *Danvers*, in favour
'of *Antipædobaptism*, are laid down, shewing the
'Vanity and Insignificancy of them, as to his
'purpose.

'First, That which offers it self to considera-
,tion is our Authors great unfaithfulness in his
,Quotations, and gross abuse of the Authors
'cited by him in favour of his cause: Sometimes
'he seems to have meerly forged Testimonies, and
'to pretend Authors to have said what he could
'wish they had; but what indeed never came
'into their Minds, much less drop'd from their
'Pens: Sometimes he grosly perverts their words,

wresting

' wresting them to suc[...]nse, as apparently
' was never intended [...]em: Sometimes he
' mistakes, and Fathers that upon one, which
' was spoken by another, &c.
But here no man can credit this Witness, &c.
' I shall only Instance in those Testimonies he
' cites out of the *Magdeburgensian* History, of
' which he gives, and that not undeservedly, a
' great *Encomium*: In the 1, 2, and 3. Centuries
' they tell us, (sayes he in his 56. Page) that as
' to the Business of Baptism in the First Century
' they find to have been after this manner, &c. As to
' the Subjects of Baptism, they tell us that in this
' Age, (meaning the First Century,) the Age where-
' in Christ and his Apostles lived, they find, that
' they baptized only the Adult or Aged, whether Jews
' or Gentiles; but as to the baptizing of Infants, they
' confess they read of no Examples. And he has
' the confidence to direct his Reader to the *Cen-*
' *tury*, *Book*, and *Page*, where he saith they tell
' us all this; whereas they are so far from telling
' us all this, that they say the direct contrary.
' That the Aged, whether Jews or Gentiles,
' were baptized, those Examples, *Acts* 2. 8, 10,
' 16, 19. prove. 'It is true, we read not of
' any Express Example of Infants being baptized:
' But that they were, even in the Apostles times,
' both *Origen* and *Cyprian*, and others of the Fa-
' thers, did Testifie; and this is also evident from
' the Writings of the Apostles themselves, and
' then they shew us, what Evidence they concei-
' ved they had from the Writings of the A-
' postles, that Infants were baptized. Now is
this to tell us, that they baptized only the A-
dult? Nay, do they not tell us expresly, that
they find from the Writings of the Apostles, and
the Testimonies of the Fathers that lived near
those

those times, that they baptized Infants, as well as grown Persons?

'*Chap. 4. pag. 48.* they say expresly, *Nec uf-*
'*quam legitur Infantes hoc Saeculo à Baptifmo Remo-*
'*tos esse*: And cites *Origen*, as affirming, that the
' Baptism of Infants had been received by the
' Church, as a Tradition from the Apostles.'
' And after the same manner does he most
' grosly abuse them, and impose upon his Reader,
' in what he cites out of them in the Third and
' Fourth *Centuries*. But it is needless to trace
' him any further, by what hath been said, we
' may see the great unfaithfulness of our Author.
Thus much for the Testimony of Mr. *Joseph Whiston*.

2. Mr. *Obed Wills* in his Book *Vindiciæ Vindiciarum*, in the Title Page saith,

An Appeal to the Baptists so called, against Mr. Danvers, for his strange Forgeries, and Misrepresentation of divers Councils and Authors, both Antient and Modern.

Page 6. saith he, *Now for Mr.* Danvers.
' Thus to Father on the *Magdiburgs* what they
' never spake, and also pervert what they did
' speak, renders him chargeable with Falshood
' and Prevarication; for (1.) they say no such
' thing, that it was the universal practice to bap-
' tize onely the Adult upon profession of Faith:
' But of this in its proper place, when we shall
' make good the Charge of Falshood against him,
' in divers other things, as well as this.

To which I must refer the Reader in his Book. Now, Sir, you could not be ignorant of these black Characters, that are given Mr. *Danvers* by these two Authors aforesaid, publickly in Print, whatever he is by others.

Therefore to allude to your own Reflection upon

on me in *Page* 3. Would any Man, but one that was almost at his Wits end, and also famished for want of good Authority to vindicate his tottering Principles by, [have] quoted such a corrupt Author as this, and value himself upon him, as he hath done! But now I bethink my self, we shall not so much need to make a wonder at it, when we find this our Author himself tardy of the same kind of practice.

13. In *Pag.* 4. this Author is pleased to mock and scoff at Habitual Faith, and Faith *potentia,* tho' not *Actu visibili,* and Believers Seed being in the Covenant.

Saith he, *For my part I think Transubstantiation, Habitual Faith, and the Infant Seed of Believers, in the Covenant, are Terms equally allowable, and probably, equally understood among their various Professors. This Habitual Faith in Infants is much of the likeness of our* Athenian *Assertion, That Infants have Faith* potentia, *though not* Actu visibili, *so you say, they have Habitual, though not Actual visible Faith.*

1. Pray mark, He will not allow of the Seed of Believers to be capable of having Habitual Faith, nor of being in the Covenant of Grace, and yet he holds, that dying Infants are saved; and if they are not in the Covenant of Grace, then they are in the Covenant of Works, and are saved in that: Which overthrows the very Foundation of the Christian Religion.

2. There is no Salvation to be had, for either young or old, out of the Covenant of Grace; therefore by his Argument all dying Infants are lost, and damned for ever; for the Scripture saith, *Eph.* 2. 8, 9. *For by grace are ye saved, through faith; and that not of your selves: it is the gift*

gift of God: Not of works, lest any man should boast.

But to proceed in the second place, Seeing this Author hath been pleased to join those Gentlemens Notion and mine together, and make us Co-partners in his Derision, in point of Honour and Reputation I will vindicate theirs, as well as my own, and leave Transubstantiation to him that can make Men Anabaptists when they are dead, that abhorred that Principle when they were alive; and we find, he is fain to be beholding to those Men of the transubstantiated Stamp for some of their Principles, to help maintain his own by, namely, in adding to, or diminishing from the Scripture *Rev.* 22. as his Opinion doth will and require, to defend it from the Truth.

1. First of all, I do positively declare, that all true saving Faith, both Habitual and Actual, in all the Elect of God, both old and young, is of one and the same Nature and Essence, which is called *Titus* 1. 1. *The faith of Gods elect*; and in *Eph.* 4. *One faith.*

2. That this Faith, that seems to lie dormant in the Soul of an Elect Infant, with a respect to any visible Activity, is of the very same nature and kind with that Faith which removes Mountains in the Soul of an Adult Believer.

3. One would have thought that no Man would ever have snarled, or derided at that Character of Faith, namely, Faith *potentia*, except it had been one that is an utter Stranger unto, and altogether unacquainted with the Nature and Excellency of that Grace.

4. Let us hear what a transcendent Character our Saviour Christ himself hath given to the very Nature of Faith, *Verily I say unto you, If ye have faith as a grain of mustard seed, ye shall say unto this mountain, Remove hence to yonder place, and it shall remove: nothing shall be impossible to you.* Mark

Mark 11. 23. *For verily I say unto you, that whosoever shall say unto this mountain, Be thou removed, and be thou cast into the sea, and shall not doubt in his heart, but shall believe that those things which he saith shall come to pass, he shall have whatsoever he saith.*

Here you see what a power there is attributed to the least Grain or Degree of Faith: Not barely *potentia*, but in a sense *omnipotentia*; nothing impossible unto it.

5. How dare Men be so bold and hardy, as to ascribe weakness to Faith, as our Authour in effect hath done, by ridiculing and scoffing at the Notion of Faith *potentia*, when there is no such thing as weakness in the Nature of Faith, though the Act of Faith is either stronger or weaker, according to the good pleasure of him that worketh all things in us, and for us, by the Influence of his Spirit, according to the counsel of his own Will.

6. Faith in its own Nature is not weak, but it is as strong and powerful in it self, in the weakest Believer, as it is in the strongest Saint upon Earth: The Grace of Faith in an Elect Infant is as strong, as in the Adult Believer: The weakness and imperfection lieth in the Creature, and not in Faith; and this weakness by Nature is alike in all. There is no more strength by Nature in an old Saint to act Faith by, than there is in an Elect dying Infant; therefore all our sufficiency is in the All-sufficient God. *For who maketh thee to differ from another? And what hast thou that thou didst not receive? Now if thou didst receive it, why dost thou glory, as if thou hadst not received it? And Christ is the Author and Finisher of our Faith, and of Eternal Salvation.*

7. And Lastly, I will lay down an Illustrating *Simily*, which shall be this, The Fire that lieth covered

covered over with Ashes upon the Hearth, and cannot be seen, is of the same Nature, Power, and Essence, with that which burneth actually upon the Hearth, or with that which acts furiously in burning down Houses, Towns, and Cities.

For if you do but stir up that fire, which lyeth dormant under the Ashes, and apply Fewel unto it, you will soon see it exercise its Power and Strength, in devouring all that it can fasten upon.

So when the wind of God's Spirit blows upon Faith, that lieth dormant, either in old or young, it will soon burn up in a flame of Love and Zeal for God; *Sol.* 4. 16. *Awake, O north-wind, and come thou south, blow upon my garden, that the spices thereof may flow out, &c.*

Pray observe what work this wind did make, even upon Children, in *Matth.* 21. 15, 16. *And when the chief priests and scribes saw the wonderful things that he did, and the children crying in the temple, and saying, Hosanna to the son of David; they were sore displeased, And said unto him, Hearest thou what these say? And Jesus saith unto them, Yea; have ye never read, Out of the mouth of babes and sucklings thou hast perfected praise?*

Here you see this Celestial fire did burn in these very Children, if you will believe our Saviour Christ; for praising God is an Act of Faith; for none can praise him without believing in him; therefore here were Children acting the Grace of Faith.

When this Celestial Fire, the Grace of Faith, which ever worketh by Love; for as Faith is the Fire, so Love is the Flame, comes to be stirred up, and Influenced by the Holy Spirit, it will quickly burn down all the strong Holds of Satan in the Soul, *viz.* All Sins both Original and Actual, and never leave burning until it hath destroyed all, and leave neither Root, nor Branch

ve the Soul until Faith be swallowed
in Glory. Therefore never open
against that Notion of Faith *potentia*

second place I shall offer something
rs consideration about Habitual Faith,
also corroborate the Notion of Faith

an Adult Believer is asleep, what
apable of acting at that time, during
ore than an Elect dying Infant is in
or in the Cradle? When a Believer
, the Grace of Faith doth not drop
eart; for *David* said, *Whenever I a-
still with thee*; that was, he was ever
d.
rve what our Saviour said unto his
parallel case, *Matth.* 26, 38; 40, 41,
Saviour Christ commanded his Dis-
ch, but they all fell asleep. 2. He
m for not obeying his Command, and
, *What could ye not watch with me one*
three times following. Where was
of Grace? Why, it was suspended,
t the Habit of Grace stood firm. As
ate of Grace, and a spiritual frame
Believers:
is the Habits of Grace belongeth to
State; and the Acts of Grace belon-
Spiritual frame of Heart:
e sleepy Disciples, though they had
of Grace, yet the Habit was secured;
id in *Mark* 14. 38. *Watch ye and pray,
into temptation: the spirit truly is ready*,
is their Spiritual state; for though
sleep, and that contrary to Christ's
yet he in his Apology for them did
demonstrate,

demonstrate, that they had the Habit of Grace in them, *but the flesh was weak.* There was no Grace in Exercise: The Spiritual frame of Heart was lost.

3. When a Believer is in a Swoon, or Trance, or distracted, (in which conditions they are not capable to act faith) doth he then lose the Habit of faith? God forbid! That is against my Principles, which was the onely Truth this Authour said of me, as I know of, in all his Book, though he did it to manage a fallacious Argument against me; but in all such cases as aforesaid, God will have Mercy and not Sacrifice.

4. This was that which relieved *Job* when he was, as it were, overwhelmed and buried in Affliction, yet Habitual faith kept his Head above Water; for he knew that his Redeemer lived, and that he had the Root of the Matter in him, *Job* 19. 25, 28. I do not believe *Job* was in the Exercise of Grace, when he cursed the Day of his Birth; for it is a Mercy we ought to bless God for.

5. When Believers fall into sin, do they lose the Habit of Grace? No. Though the Exercise of Grace be suspended, yet the Habit remains; for were it not so, no Adult Believer could possibly be saved; for we find the most Eminent Saints of all, both in Old Testament-times, and in the New, fell very foully.

1. *Noah* fell into the sin of Drunkenness. 2. *Lot* into Incest. 3. *David* fell into the sin of Adultery and Murder, and lay under the guilt of it along time, until God sent the Prophet *Nathan* to awaken him. Now he had the Habit of faith in him all the while; but when this Celestial fire was blown up, then he bewails his sin, and confesses it, and Renews his Covenant with the Lord, *Psal.* 51.   2. In

2. In new Testament time there was *Peters* Denial of Christ, and all the Apostles forsaking him just when he was going to suffer, when they should have shewn most love and affection unto him, then they most failed him; will any one dare to say that *Peter* did Act Grace, when he denyed Christ in a passion, with Cursing and Swearing, or that he had not the Habit of Faith in him at that time? surely No.

Once more, what think ye of those unworthy partakers at the Table of the Lord, the Apostle *Paul* tells us of in 1 *Cor.* 11. 29, 30. they were Believers, they were in a Spiritual State, but in a Carnal Frame of heart: *For this cause many are weak and sickly among you, and many sleep,* among you who? why among you Believers, they died for profaning the Lords Table; these were Habitual Believers, but they were unworthy receivers, and cannot Habitual Faith carry an Elect dying Infant to Heaven and Glory, as well as Adult Believers, thus I hope by this time our Author hath gotten some knowledge, and understanding of the Notion of Habitual Faith, which he confessed himself so much a stranger unto.

6. And Lastly, What are the ends and designs of the Exercise of Grace?

1. To this I answer, first, in the General it is to Glorify God, *Let your Light so shine before men, that they which see your good works may gloryfie your Father which is in Heaven.*

2. Believers do glorifie God in these ways, and in the performance of these Duties, following.

1. By Watching against Satan, and repelling his Temptation by Faith and Prayer, *Eph.* 6. 16. 18.

2. In Watching against the Allurements of the World, and over our own hearts, to overcome them

them both; in kee——g them asunder as you would Fire and Gunpowder, which no sooner touch but take.

3. By subduing all Acts of Unbelief.

4. By Watching against the rising up and Rebellion of the remainders of Inbred Corruption.

5. By continual Prayer to God through Christ, to be delivered from all sin whatsoever known, or not known by us, that God would discover it unto us, and pardon it in the Blood of Christ.

6. Be diligent and vigilant to keep up Communion with God, and be sure to watch in special manner, after you have met with great Emanation of the Spirit in Communion with God for that is that which Satans malice rages most against a Believer for.

7. In Watching for the coming of Christ, and the Destruction of Antichrist, and the Conversion of the *Jews*.

8. And Lastly, the Exercise of Grace lyeth much in being earnest Suiters at the Throne of Grace for fresh supplies of Grace; to be found walking in Gods ways, in keeping close to his Ordinances, and pure institutions according to Gods own appointment, and not of Mens inventing; and in obedience of all Gods Commandments. Now we have need of Faith, as the Scripture saith: for the Grace that serves for the performance of one Duty, will not be sufficient for the performance of another, as we cannot live to Day by the Bread we had Yesterday: But as we must have dayly supplys of Bread for our Bodies, so we must for the supply of our Souls: For Grace is the Souls Spiritual Bread, and especially the Grace of Faith, For it is said *now the just shall live by Faith*, Hab. 2. 4. Heb. 10. 38.

Now

Now as an Elect dying Infant cannot Exercise Grace in an ordinary way, as is required of an Adult Believer; so on the other hand, he hath not that occasion as an Adult Believer hath? What occasion hath an Elect dying Babe of the exercise of Grace, that never committed any actual sin; for he cannot be tempted to sin by the devices of Satan, nor be led away by the allurements of the World, for all the Duty he is to perform, is Passive: And therefore Habitual Faith is sufficient to perform Passive Duties, for all the sin he hath to subdue is original: And I have sufficiently shewn both how, and who doth that for them, and in them, and there is nothing required of an Elect dying Infant personally, but passive Obedience, and therefore that Ordinance in which all the Subjects are Passive, doth properly and chiefly belong to them and not to the Adult, unless they were Adult Heathens, that should be proselyted to the Christian Religion, namely, Baptism, it doth belong principally to these Passive obedient Church-members, tho' Relatively they are Active, because Christ hath done all for them personally. Thus you see I have made good the Notion of Habitual Faith.

14. Now Sir, I must begin to attack you in the most sensible parts, and I cannot avoid it, you have charged me falsly and Clandestinely, with setting my self in a posture of War against God, and of being an Advocate against the Truth.

In Page 1. in these words, *What is this man Resolved to set himself in a posture of War against God, and his Word?* &c.

What can be expected, when a man shall be an Advocate against the Truth.

Here you have craftily by a side Wind charged
me

me with Rebellion against God; but you have not proved it upon me.

Therefore I challenge you to prove your charge, for if you do not, as I am sure you cannot, then you will prove your self to be the man *David* spake of as you say of me in, Page 11. *that Travelleth with iniquity, conceiveth mischief and brought forth falshood.* It is no new thing for persons to charge that upon others, which they themselves are guilty of; but it is as old as *Nero*.

But had I dealt by the holy Scriptures as you have done, which will appear in two Instances, especially I should have been guilty of Spiritual Rebellion, and High Treason also: But what you are guilty of, I will leave to the Reader to judge.

1. I will begin with the first Instance, in Page 5. where you had laboured very industriously to Invalid inherent Faith, and the extent of the free Grace of God to Elect dying Infants, and to justifie your own Lame Decrepit way of Salvation for them, without the Grace of Faith, where you had occasion to quote that Text, in *Eph.* 2. 8, 9. the words in our Bible are as followeth, *For by grace are ye saved, through Faith; and that not of your selves: it is the gift of God. Not of works lest any man should boast.*

2. But you say, *By grace are ye saved through faith: Not of works, lest any man should boast.* Pray mind the subtilty and fallacy of this Man: For rather than he will part with his Opinion, he will part with that Truth that doth oppose it. Pray mind, for it is worth your Observation, for he hath cut the 8 Verse in two, and took the 9 Verse, and fine drawed it on to the former part of the 8 Verse, and it is done so cleverly, that there is nothing to be discerned, but that it's all but one Verse; for he hath brought it on the same Line, without any

any, &c. juſt as if it was but one Verſe; but what he hath done with the latter part of the 8 Verſe, I know not, for he hath clipt it quite off. But,

3. He had Reaſon enough for it, ſuch as it was, though none of the beſt; for the Text tells us, that *faith is not of our ſelves: It is the gift of God*: And if ſo, then God may give it unto whom he pleaſe; he is not confined to beſtow it upon none, but upon Perſons that are qualified to receive it by Maturity of Years; though this Author will have it, that faith ſtands in the wiſdom of Men; for he will not allow, that young Infants are capable of receiving of it, which proves the Conſequence clearly: but all that are ſaved, both old and young, are ſaved through the Grace of faith in Chriſt Jeſus. Again,

4. The management of this Text of Scripture is very appoſite and agreeable to that new Doctrine of our Authors, that ſaith, That all Adult Believers are ſaved by the Righteouſneſs of Chriſt, through faith, and that dying Infants are ſaved by the ſame Righteouſneſs, without faith, which he calls their Better way, &c.

5. If God's Grace ſaves freely, and is at God's diſpoſal fully, then God may beſtow it upon whom he pleaſe, and with-hold it from whom he pleaſeth, and who ſhall find fault with the Diſpenſations of God's Grace? for he is a Debtor to none of his Creatures, but he is Arbitrary in the diſpenſing of all his Graces.

6. But this Text aforeſaid, taken in its full Scope and Latitude, doth deſtroy the very Vitals of their Opinion, and overthrows the very foundation of it, *viz*. That Infants are not capable of receiving the Grace of faith; and therefore, ſaith our Author, they have nothing to do to meddle with Gods moſt Holy Things, unleſs they have

perſonal

personal Actual Faith: And if they have nothing to do with God's most Holy Things, then they can never be saved; for no unclean thing shall enter into Heaven; *for without holiness no man shall see the Lord:* For all Children are conceived in a state of sin and unbelief, and nothing but the Grace of faith, in the Hand of the Spirit, can change that state; for if that state be not changed there is no possibility of being saved: *For without faith it is impossible to please God.*

7. Again, The natural Consequences of his Doctrine are as followeth, (1.) That God cannot work faith in young Infants, because they are not able to help him, which doth reflect great Dishonour upon the Power of God's Omnipotent free Grace, and mightily lessens that. (2.) It doth tacitely declare, that God is not able to make them capable of the Reception of his Grace, because they are not of Years to exercise it. Hath this Authour never read, that *out of the mouth of babes and sucklings God hath perfected praise*, Mat. 21. 16. Psal. 8. 2. Those Scriptures carry a very great weight in them: Me-thinks you should study the depth of them, and get Acquaintance with them, and they would convince you, that Children are capable of receiving Grace; for these Children did act Grace, and it was God that did perfect it in them. (3.) A Third Consequence is, That Adult Persons do qualifie themselves for the Reception of Grace, or at least wise, are Co-partners with the Spirit of Grace in the working of it. (4.) If this be so, then it is not God's Grace, but Man's Works; No, nor Faith is not God's Gift, but Man's Merit. But now pray observe how the Apostle doth argue this Point in *Rom.* 11. 6. *And if by grace, then it is no more of works: otherwise grace is no more grace. But if it be of works,*
then

then it is no more grace : otherwise work is no more work. These two Texts of Scripture, that of *Eph.* 2. 8, 9. and that of *Rom.* 11. 6. and Anabaptism cannot stand together, they are incompatible. You said you had got me in the Pound, in Page 5. but if I were, yet now I am gotten out, and you are in the Pound your self, or at least you have taken a *Tartar*.

15. Now, Sir, I am come to prove the Second Instance upon you; for as you have diminished the Word of God in the former Instance; so here you have added unto it : I chuse rather to say so, than to call it clipping and coyning, because it is the softest Terms that it can be drest in, that is any way suitable unto such a foul practice, though there is a dreadful Threatning that doth attend it, *Rev.* 22. 18, 19. *Deut.* 4. 2. *Prov.* 30. 6. The Lord make you truly sensible of the evil of it, and grant you Repentance unto Life, which is the worst hurt that I desire may befal you, in all that I say unto you, or of you.

In Page 13. you say,

Arg. 3. *The promise of Remission of sin, and the gift of the holy Ghost, unto the Children of Believers is upon the terms of Repentance, and obedience, Ergo the promise is not to the Fleshly and natural Seed of Believers as such.*

1. Whatever that promise was to *Abraham* and his Seed ; it is the same to the Gentile Believers and their Seed, And *Acts* 2. 39. doth clearly make it appear to be so : *For the promise is unto you, and to your Children, and to all that are afar off, even as many as the Lord our God shall call* : here both *Jew* and *Gentile* and their Seed, are comprehended in the promise, *Eph.* 3. 6. *That the Gentiles should*

should be fellow-heirs, and of the same body, and partakers of his promise in Christ by the Gospel.

What is this Body, which is called the same Body? Why it is the myftical Body of Chrift, the Church which the *Jews* were in; and to partake of the promife that was *Abrahams* promife in Chrift by the Gofpel: for *Abraham* had the Gofpel preached unto him, under the Difpenfation of the Law, *Gal.* 3. 8. Here you fay the promife of Remiffion of fin, and the gift of the Holy Ghoft unto the Children of Believers is upon the terms of Repentance and Obedience: fo that if they perform thefe conditions perfonally, then they fhall be pardoned and converted. But how doth this agree with the free Grace of God, for Chrift is a Prince and Saviour to give Repentance unto Life, and to give Remiffion of fin, for it is he alone that worketh all our works in us; and how do this agree with this Scripture, *Phil.* 2. 13. *For it is God that worketh in you, both to will and to do of his good pleafure*, fo that by your Doctrine no dying Infant can be faved, becaufe they cannot perform the terms: and fo to exclude them from Baptifm you exclude them from Heaven at the fame time and how can Children be fit for the Kingdom of Heaven as you faid, if they muft perform the Conditions perfonally. But I have told you already who hath performed all the Conditions of the Covenant for Elect dying Infants, and fo he doth for Adult Believers too, or elfe they would come fhort of Heaven and Glory, read *Rom.* 5. 17, 18, 19, 20. *Rom.* 8. 33, 34. 1 *Cor.* 15. 21, 22. Here you fee who it is that hath done all thefe things for them.

And as for Believers Seed, both Spiritual and Carnal: now under the Gofpel they have as good an Intereft in the Covenant which God made with
Abraha

Abraham, as ever Believers Seed both Spiritual and Carnal, enjoyed under the Law of *Moses,* what tho' we have not an Interest in the Land of Canaan, yet we have that which is equivalent, *Mat.* 6 33. *Rom.* 8. 32.

I should not have meddled with this Argument in particular, because it will fall with the rest, had it not been to have shewn how unfaithfully you have dealt with the Scriptures, which you made use of to prove this Argument by: But I would have answered this with all the rest of your lame Arguments together, in what I have yet farther to say.

Let all the World behold and see how you have dealt with the Scripture in *Acts* 2. 38, 39. But it is on the 39 Verse you have done the feat. I cannot relate these things without great Regret of Spirit. You begin with part of the 37 Verse, *Men and brethren, what shall we do? Peter answered them, Repent and be baptized in the name of Jesus Christ, for the remission of sins, and ye shall receive the gift of the holy Ghost.*

For this promise is unto you, and your children also, yea and to the very Gentiles afar of, if they are called.

Reader this is Printed in a distinct Character for Canonical Scripture, with that part which is True, therefore pray mind the difference.

Verse 39. *For the promise is unto you, and to your Children, and to all that are afar off, even as many as the Lord our God shall call:* that was to all the Elect Gentiles and their Children; for the promise runs in the very same Channel to the Gentiles and their Children in the Text, without any variation, as it did to the *Jews* and their Children.

1. But here our Authour coyned the Word [*this promise,*] whereas it is said [*the promise.*]

2. He saith, [*to you and your children also,*] whereas it is said, [*unto you, and to your children.*]

3. Saith he, [*yea to the very Gentiles afar off,* [*if*] *they are called,*] whereas it is written thus, viz. [*And to* [*all*] *'that are afar off, even as many as the Lord our God* [*shall*] *call.*]

Pray Reader observe;. This Authour hath endeavoured to change the very Frame of the Covenant, in which the Promise stands; for whereas the Holy Spirit saith, *the promise,* he hath said, *this promise.*

The Promise is that which doth belong to the Everlasting Covenant, which God made with *Abraham* and his Seed in their Generations, *Exod.* 19. 5. *Psal.* 89. 28. to Verse 34. For there was no Salvation under the Law, but what was conveyed unto them through that Promise, nor under the Gospel neither. But *this promise* suits well with his Dissolution of the Covenant; and therefore to bring his Marks to bear, it must be *this promise,* as if it had been some new made Promise, that never had been in being, nor declared before. For he saw that the Gentiles, and their Children, were included in [*the*] *promise,* and made Partakers of all the Covenant Priviledges, as the believing Jews and their Children were, who were the People which the Apostle spake this unto; therefore he saith, *Yea to the very Gentiles afar off,* [*if*] *they are called,* when the Text saith plainly thus, viz, *And to all that are afar off, even as many as the Lord our God shall call*; and not [*if*] *they are called:* By which he makes it a dubious, precarious thing, Whether they would be called or not; whereas they were to be fellow-heirs with the believing Jews, *Eph.* 3. 6. But the grand

Reason

Reason of all this is very plain and obvious, which was this, namely, because he would not have the Christian Gentiles, and their Children, to share with the Believing *Hebrews*, and their Children, in the promise:

For that would have spoiled his design of Dissolving and Repealing the Covenant; and so to cut off and cast out the Infant Seed of Believers from all the Priviledges of the Covenant; that so these poor Babes might not have a right to the Ordinance of Baptism, the Initiating Seal or token of the Covenant. Now for the Conclusion of this Head.

Pray Reader take notice of this Reflection of our Author's upon me.

In Page 2. saith he, *Tis certainly an Argument of profound Confidence, for a Man to pretend to the world the Discovery of the Errours of a People, whose Principles he knows no more comparatively, then I know* Utopia.

To this I answer thus, Suppose I allow and grant what he hath said to be true; that I am thus ignorant of their Principles, as he Represents me to be.

Yet I must tell him, that I am not altogether ignorant of their Devices and Stratagems, by which they uphold their Opinion; in which their Principles are enveloped and lye Dormant.

But before I have done with this Treatise, it may be I may make him and some others of that Leaven, sensible that I am not so much a stranger to their Principles as well as their Errours as he would make the world believe I am.

16. In Page 11. saith our Author;
Now I come to your challenge in your Book, page 12. And here he repeats my Challenge.

I chal-

I challenge all the Anabaptists in the world, to produce but one plain Text of Scripture, either in the old Testament or the new, from Gen. 17. to the very last of Revelations; to prove that ever the Children of Believing Parents were cast out of Covenant, by any authority from God, and I will submit unto them.

But saith the good Man.

My fear is this person is so prepossest, that all a man can say, tho' never so much to the purpose, it will not be regarded.

To this I answer, he saith very right indeed in that he hath said, *all that a man can say, tho' never so much to the purpose will not be regarded*; no nor what all the Men of your Opinion can say, with all the Women to help them neither: as long as God hath not said it. One [*thus saith the Lord*] is infinitely more worth than all a Man can say; but it is so far from [*thus saith the Lord,*] as that the Lord hath not only said the contrary, but hath Sworn to it, that the covenant which he made with *Abraham* and his Seed, is an everlasting Covenant; and therefore it cannot be Dissolved nor taken up by the Roots, *Psal.* 105. 8, 9. *He hath remembred his Covenant for ever, the word which he commanded to a thousand generations.*

Which Covenant he made with Abraham, and his oath unto Isaac.

Psal. 89. 34, 35. *My Covenant will I not break, nor alter the thing that is gone out of my lips.*

Once have I sworn by my holiness that, I will not lie unto David.

Therefore as long as God hath not only said it, but also sworn it; it matters not to me what *a man saith*, but let God be true, and man a liar: and for this Reason I am so far from submitting unto what *a man saith*, as that I do in the name of the Lord

Lord in vindication of the honour and glory, of his moſt *Sacred Oath*, reſume my Challenge.

Firſt of all our Saviour Chriſt did ſo demonſtrate his tender Love, and affection unto the Children of Believers, in his ſweet carriage and behaviour towards them; when he was perſonally upon Earth, in his taking them up in his Arms, and in his laying his Hands on them, and Bleſſing them, and Praying for them; and not only ſo, but he declared that of ſuch was the Kingdom of Heaven, that is the Church; and in that Chriſt did conſequentially declare them to be Members of the Church.

This was ſuch a demonſtration of Love and Grace to little Children, as cannot be parallell'd in all the old Teſtament. Surely then, Chriſt would never have ſhewed them ſo much favour, if they had been caſt out of Covenant, or cut off from Church-Memberſhip; when he declared that the Church were of ſuch Members: The Priviledges of the Covenant which God made with *Abraham* do as much belong to all the Seed of Goſpel-Believers, as ever they did to the Seed of Believers under the *Moſaick* Law: as I ſhall clearly make it appear by and by.

2. *You have here the anſwer of my challenge as he* ſaith, *ſuch a one as it is*; therefore I pray you to take good Notice of it: *Your demand is that we prove Infants Incovenanting, and the priviledges Children once had with their Parents Repealed.*

1. *Therefore that the Covenant of peculiarity made to Abraham and his natural Seed; as ſuch is aboliſhed I prove from theſe* 4 or 5 *Arguments following*, &c.

The natural Branches are broken off, Ergo, *Childrens viſible Incovenanting is Repealed*, the Antecedent of this Enthymem is clear from the Apoſtles Aſſertion,

tion, Rom. 11. 19, 20, 21. *The branches were broken off: By the Natural Branches, without controverſie, is to be underſtood the natural Seed of* Abraham.

But before we do enter farther into the Controverſie, I muſt put the Reader in mind of Two Things.

1. Is this that he hath not told us; Who it was that made this Covenant of Peculiarity with *Abraham*, whether it was God or Man, in all his Book: Though he hath many times cited the Notion occaſionally, it may as well be ſome Covenant about his own private Affairs, between himſelf and ſome other Perſon, either between him and his Steward, or Herdſmen, or Tenants, or about ſome Houſes or Land, or I know not what it was; but it was a Covenant of Peculiarity to *Abraham* and his Natural Seed.

2. He hath not laid down the Everlaſting Covenant, which God made with *Abraham* and his Seed in their Generation, in all his Book, altho' he hath mentioned the Chapter and Verſe wherein it is twice, in Page 14. *Gen.* 17. 7. There is another cunning Device; but his Pen would not write againſt the Hand that guided it.

2. But to proceed in the ſecond place to the Controverſy. You ſay the natural Branches are broken off: *Ergo*, Childrens viſible Incovenanting is repealed, &c.

And he farther ſaith, That this Covenant is taken up by the Roots, and the Natural Branches broken off, none excepted.

3. You ſay the Natural Branches are broken off: *Ergo*, Childrens viſible Incovenanting is repealed. Now, Sir, you ſhall ſee that this doth no more prove, That the Children of believing Parents were

were caft out of the Everlafting Covenant, which God made with *Abraham* and his Seed in their Generations, than the Barrennefs of the *Effex* Jail-Keepers proved that the converted Jaylor, in *Acts* 16: had no Children belonging to his Family.

4. And Laftly, This is the Foundation on which you have built all your Florid, Syllogiftical Arguments: And if I can deftroy this Foundation, then will all your Building fall, and great will be the *Fall* thereof; therefore I fhall not begin on the Top of the Houfe, but I will undermine your Foundation, and blow it up all at once. If a Man be to cut down a Tree by the Roots, he would not climb up on Top of the Tree, and fall a lopping off the Branches thereof, branch by branch, when his work and bufinefs lyeth at the Root: So here, by God's affiftance, I will cut down this Tree by the Roots of it, and then your Book will be fully Anfwered. What though the Arguments may be rightly formed, and materially good in themfelves, yet if they are deducted from wrong Topicks, and built upon a Rotten Foundation, and applyed to wrong Subjects, then they are all naught, even like *Jeremiah*'s Figs, that were fo vile that they could not be eaten; or like a very fair Houfe, that is built upon a Sandy foundation, that as foon as a Storm comes down it tumbles.

-The Law of God againft Blafphemy is very good in it felf, whenever it is rightly applyed; but as the Jews malicioufly applyed it to our Saviour Chrift, fo it was not; for faid they, *We have a law, and by our law he ought to die, becaufe he made himfelf the Son of God.* Now if any other Perfon had affirmed this of himfelf, (but Chrift,)

Chrift,) it had been blafphemy in them, and the Jews had been right. Or,

2. They are like your own Argument, which you raifed againft me upon that notorious falfe Charge, *viz.* That I have afferted in my Book, without mentioning any Page, That all the Children of Believers have Habitual Faith : Your Argument is rightly formed, and materially good in it felf, but being built on a falfe, rotten foundation, it renders it a meer Nonentity; and fo are all your Arguments, which you have produced to prove the Diffolution of the Covenant, and of the Children of believing Parents being caft out of Covenant by the coming of the Gofpel : They are but meer, fictitious, empty Notions ; for the very Text you have pitched upon is againft you, and inftead of miniftring any kind of Relief unto you, will but entangle you.

If any Man can make the breaking off fome of the Branches, and the grafting of others in the room, to be a taking the Covenant up by the Roots, as you affert in *Page* 14. I muft confefs he muft be a better Logician than I am.

Now having thus premifed thefe things, and made way for what I have to offer, I proceed.

1. We muft confider what this Olive Tree is in *Rom.* 11.
2. Who thefe Branches were, which were broken off.
3. We muft confider how they came to be broken off.
4. We muft confider who they were that were graffed in, which our Author takes no notice of.
5. And Laftly, How they came to be graffed in. I take

1. I take this Olive Tree to be Christ, whom God gave to be a Covenant to the People, or Christ Mystical the Church; but then it may be Objected, How can any Branches, that are in Christ, be broken off? Why our Saviour Christ himself hath Answered this Objection to our Hands, *John* 15. 2. *Every branch in me that beareth not fruit, he taketh away: and every branch that beareth fruit, he purgeth it, that it may bring forth more fruit.*

Rom. 11. 17. *And if some of the branches be broken off,* &c.

Thus you see this Olive Tree is Christ, the Covenant; and he is not taken up by the Roots, nor dissolved.

2. These Branches, which were broken off, were some of the unbelieving Jews, and all their Posterity: It were but some of the Branches that were broken off from the Olive Tree, the Covenant remaineth untouched.

3. How came the Jews to be broken off? *Rom.* 11. 20. tells us, That it was because of unbelief they were broken off, *&c.*

4. The Gentiles were graffed into the same Olive Tree, in their Room, *Rom.* 11. 17. *And if some of the branches be broken off, and thou being a wild olive tree, wert graffed in amongst them, and with them partakest of the root and fatness of the olive-tree.* As those Jews, which were these Branches that were broken off, and their Children with them were cast out of the Covenant, so the Gentiles, and all their Children, were taken into Covenant in their room, and did partake of the same Priviledges with those Jews that did abide firm in the Covenant; for the Text tells us, that they were graffed in amongst them, and did partake of the root and fatness of the Olive-tree:

D 4   The

the Gentiles were made fellow-heirs with the *Jews*, *Eph*. 3. 6. And in *Acts* 2. 39. there the holy Ghost hath joyned *Jew* and Gentile, and their Children together in the Promise of the everlasting Covenant which God made with *Abraham*, *Gen*. 17. 7. *And I will establish my Covenant between me and thee, and thy seed after thee, in their generations, for an everlasting Covenant ; to be a God unto thee, and to thy seed after thee.*

5. And Lastly, the Gentiles and their Seed were graffed into Christ, the Covenant by Faith ; for as the *Jews* and their Children were cast out of the Covenant by their unbelief, (so) on the other hand, the Gentiles were taken in by Faith, *Rom*. 11. 20. *Well ; because of unbelief they were broken off, and thou standest by faith. Be not highminded, but fear.* This Text may refer to the *Jews* that stood principally.

Having thus stated the matter, I shall proceed on farther by Expostulation.

1. It is said the Branches are broken off, not the Tree, namely the Covenant (that) remains untouched still.

2. It were but some of the superfluous withered Branches that were broken off, not (all) the Branches. And what dammage did this do to the Tree? It made the Tree stand the firmer, and became the more Fruitfull.

3. What though some of the Branches were broken off, yet there were other Branches graffed into the Tree in their room; and is [this] to destroy the Tree : Namely to dissolve or repeal the Covenant, like an old Act of Parliament which is become useless, *Rom*. 11. 17. *And if some of the branches be broken off, and thou being a wild Olive tree, wert graffed in amongst them, and with them partakest of the root and fatness of the Olive-tree.*

Now

Now I will appeal to any experienced Christian even of their own Party to judge whether there can be a Text of Scripture produced in the whole Book of God, more full and clear, to prove the Continuation and Stability of the Covenant; after the coming in of the Gospel, and also of the taking the Gentiles and all their Seed, into the same Covenant with the *Jews* and their Seed, and of their partaking of all the same priviledges with them; who never were cast out of Covenant: then this I have laid down.

And thou being a wild Olive-tree wert graffed in amongst them; those were the Gentiles graffed in amongst the *Jews*, and with them partakest of the Root and Fatness of the Olive-tree; that were all the same priviledges with the *Jews* and their Children.

They were taken out of *Adams* broken Covenant, that wild Olive-tree; and were planted into the everlasting Covenant, which God made with *Abraham* and his Seed: Therefore whatsoever the priviledges of that Covenant afforded to the *Jews* and their Children, both under the Law and the Gospel; it is the same to all the Gentile Believers and all their Children. But besides it is Non-sence for to say, that the believing Gentiles Children were cast out of Covenant if they never were in. Pray observe our Authors Text, and observe how he hath managed it, *Rom.* 11. 19, 20, 21. The natural Branches are broken off, *Ergo* childrens visible Incovenanting is Repealed, but the 19. Verse runs thus: *Thou wilt say then, the Branches were broken off, that I might be graffed in.*

' Doth this look like a Dissolution of the Cove-
' nant State? Saith our Author, the Branches are
' broken off: By the natural branches without controversie

"troverfie is to be underftood of the natural
" Seed of Abraham.

Here you may obferve the Man was in great hafte being greedy of his prey, he could not ftay to take the Remainder of the Verfe along with him; but he had a Reafon for (that) becaufe it would have fpoiled his purpofe, for that tells you of graffing in of the Gentiles in their room, and fo the 21. Verfe tells us of the Gentiles being in, when it is faid, *For if God fpared not the natural Branches, take heed leſt he alſo ſpare not thee.* Was there ever fuch Legerdemain played with the Sacred Scriptures as this.

Now fee another Appofit Text in this *Rom.* 11. 16. *For if the firſt Fruit be holy, the lump is alſo holy: and if the root be holy, ſo are the Branches.* Now can any thing be clearer fpoken of the Continuance of *Abrahams* Covenant, the firſt Fruit the *Jews*, *viz.* the lump or whole Nation of them; and here is the fame Root on which the Gentiles are graffed, ftands firm.

Now Sir, you fee I have deftroyed all the Arguments of your whole Book already. But however I will give you farther fatisfaction. If you have not enough, you fhall have enough before I have done.

I am vindicating the Honour of my Lord and Mafters everlafting Covenant, therefore you muſt bear with me, for I fhall not fow Pillows under your Elbows.

4. Sir, you are grievoufly miftaken for to conceive that all the *Jews* and their Children were broken off, and caft out of Covenant, or that the Covenant was taken up by the Roots as you boldly affert in Page 12. which is bordering upon blafphemy, if not the thing it felf. For God faith it is an everlafting Covenant and cannot be

broken,

broken; but you say it is dissolved and taken up by the Roots: Now what is this but to make God a liar by Contradiction; and if that be not bordering upon blasphemy, What is?

1. The Text in *Rom.* 11. 17. tells us that some of the branches were broken off. For what were all the *Hebrews* to whom the Apostle writ that Epistle, but Christian Believers that were Converted from Judaism to the Christian Faith? And pray look into your very Text, which you have chosen to prove the Dissolution of the Covenant; and that may convince you of the contrary.

2. The Apostle counted them ignorant persons that did think that all the *Jews* were cast out and cut off; and Consequentially the Covenant Dissolved and pluckt up by the Roots, when some of the natural Branches were broken off, for blindness was happened but in part to *Israel*, Rom. 11. 25. *For I would not, brethren, that ye should be ignorant of this mystery, lest ye should be wise in your own conceits, that blindness in part is happened to Israel, until the fulness of the Gentiles be come in.*

3. Will any dare to say that it were onely the *Jews* Children that were cast out, and onely Adult believing Gentiles taken into the Covenant which God made with *Abraham*; for so it must be if none but Adult Believers are now in the Covenant.

Indeed if the *Anabaptists* could prove such a thing as this, then they would do their business: But without they can do this, it cannot be done; they may apply themselves to *Ezek.* 18. 20. and see if that will help them.

4. How could the breaking off of some of the Jews, and the taking in some of the Gentiles in their room, be the Dissolution of the Covenant?

For

For as the unbelieving Jews, and all their Children, only were cast out of Covenant, so the believing Gentiles, and all their Children, were taken in; for we find it was Limb for Limb, or Branch for Branch, and as all the Sprigs and Leaves, and Fruit of the Branches of the one were cast out, so on the other hand, all the Sprigs and Leaves, and Fruit of the other Branches were taken in, as all the unbelieving Jews, and all their Children, were cast out, so all the believing Gentiles, and their Children were taken in, and so remain in Covenant to this Day, and that without any alteration of the Terms thereof in the least degree, to either old or young; only it is under a new Dispensation, to what it was under the Law, and that the Jews were under long before the Gentiles were taken into covenant, which was not until after Chrifts Ascension; for the Gentiles were those Sheep which our Saviour Christ said did belong to the same Fold, or Church which the Jews were then Actual Members of, which were to be called, and converted, *John* 10. They were Sheep in Election.

5. Pray mind the Apostles Expostulation, by which he confirms the Truth aforesaid, *Rom.* 11. *I say then, hath God cast away his people? God forbid. For I also am an Israelite of the seed of Abraham, of the tribe of Benjamin. God hath not cast away his people which he foreknew*, &c.

Even so then at this present time also, there is a Remnant according to the Election of Grace.

It seems by the Apostle, as if there were some Persons among the Gentiles, in his time, that were of Opinion, that God had totally rejected and cast off all the Jews, and broken and dissolved the Covenant which he made with *Abraham* and his Seed; and the Apostle to convince them of this *Error*, takes this course, and uses this Argument,

gument, That he himself was of the Seed of *Abraham*; He pleaded his Covenant Relation to *Abraham*, And *therefore do you not believe that God hath cast out all his* Israel *out of Covenant : Do not you see me in it still, who am an* Israelite, *and of the Seed of* Abraham? As if he had said, For if all *Israel* had been cast out of Covenant, then the Apostle himself must have been cast out too.

Verse 17. *And if some of the branches be broken off, and thou being a wild olive-tree, wert graffed in among them, and with them partakest of the root and fatness of the olive-tree,* &c.

Now I will take all three of the Verses, which our Author pitched upon for his Topick, to prove the Dissolution of the Covenant, for the confirmation of the continuance thereof, both to Jew and Gentile, without straining them in the least, but as they are spontaneously in themselves, *Rom.* 11. 19, 20, 21. *Thou wilt then say, The branches were broken off, that I might be graffed in.*

Well; because of unbelief they were broken off, and thou standest by faith: Be not high minded, but fear.

This was a Caution the Apostle gave the Gentiles, that were taken into Covenant, in the room of the unbelieving Jews, which were cast out.

For if God spared not the natural branches, (these were the Jews) *take heed lest he also spare not thee.* If the Gentiles sinned as the Jews did, God would cast them out as well as he had done the Jews. Thus you see what our Authors Text affords: It is so far from proving the Dissolution of the Covenant, as that it proves the clear contrary.

6. If our Children are not in Covenant as well as we that are Believers, then we do not partake of the Root and Fatness of the Olive-tree with, and amongst the Jews, as these believing Jews did: For these believing Hebrews, which remained

mained in Covenant, all their Children remained in Covenant with them, and did partake of the root and fatness of the Covenant, or Olive-Tree.

7. Pray observe what kind of Absurdities would follow if it be not so.

(1.) How strange would it have looked for the believing Gentiles Children to be left out of the Covenant, when their Parents were taken in, and the Jews Children to remain in, with their believing Parents?

(2.) What would have become of the Promise, to both Jew and Gentile, and their Children, in *Acts* 2. 38, 39.?

(3.) And *Eph.* 2. 11. *Wherefore remember that ye being in time passed Gentiles in the flesh, who are called uncircumcision by that which is called the circumcision in the flesh made by hands;*

Verse 12. *That at that time ye were without Christ, being aliens from the common-wealth of Israel, and strangers from the covenants of promise, having no hope, and without God in the world:*

Verse 13. *But now in Christ Jesus, ye who sometimes were far off, are made nigh by the blood of Christ.*

Verse 14. *For he is our peace, who hath made both one, and hath broken down the middle wall of partition between us.*

Here you see clearly that the Jews and Gentiles are united in *Abraham*'s Covenant, and that the Gentiles, that are Believers, and all their Children, do now partake, or ought to partake of the very same Priviledges as the believing Hebrews and their Children did, is as clear as the Sun: See *Acts* 2. 39. *For the promise is unto you, and to your children, and to all that are afar off, even as many as the Lord our God shall call.* Eph. 3. 6. *That the Gentiles should be fellow-heirs, and of the same body,*

and

and partakers of his promise in Christ, by the Gospel.

Here you see both Jew and Gentile are incorporated into one Body, and from hence we may observe, That the Covenant God made with *Abraham*, and all his Seed, with all the Promises and Priviledges thereunto belonging, are devolved upon the believing Gentiles, and all their Seed and Off-spring, in the full Latitude thereof.

Therefore the Everlasting Covenant, which God made with *Abraham*, is not dissolved, nor repealed like an old, useless Act of Parliament, but stands in full Force and Vertue to this Day; and the Promises thereof run as fresh, and tast as sweet, as when God set them first abroach.

What though some of the Jews and their Children, were broken off, and cast out? The Covenant was not broken on God's part; for he took the Gentile Believers, and their Children into the Covenant, which made good the Breach; for they make the same Figure, both in Church and Covenant, and do partake of the same Benefits and Priviledges, as they did; therefore our Children must either be circumcized or baptized; but the former being abolished, it must be the latter: Wherefore let believing Parents live in the neglect of this Duty, with a respect to their Children, any longer if they dare, at their peril be it.

8. The Jews were not so careless, nor indifferent about their Children, after they themselves were converted and united to Christ, but that they would retain their old Seal and Token of the Covenant to their Children, or something equivalent in the room thereof, and never have parted with it, without an express Command from God so to do, especially if we do but consider Two

(1.) How hard a thing it was for to bring them off from Circumcision, *Acts* 15. 1, 10.

(2.) Circumcision belonged to none of the Adult Jews after the first Institution of that Ordinance, but unto their Eighth Day Children, because they were to be cut off and destroyed, if they were not circumcised at that time, *Gen.* 17. 14.

9. Would it not have been an absurd thing for to see the believing Jews baptized themselves, and their Eighth Day Children circumcized at the same time? For thus it must have been.

(2.) Would it not have been as absurd also, to see believing proselited Gentiles baptized, and no more notice taken of their Children, which are a part of themselves, than if they were Dogs, neither to circumcize them, nor baptize them? Whereas God makes no difference, now under the Gospel, between believing Jews, and believing Gentiles, as the Apostle telleth us in *Acts* 15. 8, 9. *And God which knoweth the hearts, bare them witneſs, giving them the holy Ghoſt, even as he did unto us:*

And put no difference between us and them, purifying their hearts by faith. Pray mind, It is God that purifieth the hearts, both of *Jew* and Gentile, young and old.

So that we find no alteration of the terms of the Covenant, which God made with *Abraham* and his Seed, neither to old or young; tho' it hath passed through various dispensations, and will yet do: for the Gentiles and their Seed that are in the Covenant, do partake of the same Root and Fatness of the Olive-tree, as the believing *Jews* and their Children did: It is Gods antient Land Mark, and therefore let men have a care, that endeavour to remove it.

This

This Author saith in his Book, that it is well that I am not the peoples Eyes; but I fear that those people lye under a Judgment that have such Eyes to see for them, as can see no better to distinguish about the everlasting Covenant which God made with *Abraham*, then he hath done.

17. Would it not look very absurdly for believing *Jews* Children to be Baptized; and be in the Covenant with their Parents, and not the Children of believing Gentiles: for you see there were but a part of the *Jews* broken off, and not so much as a Sprig or Leaf, or any of the Fruit broken off from the believing *Jews* that stood; and there was but a part of the Gentiles taken in, and not one Sprig, Leaf, or any of the Fruit of them left out.

Now suppose a Man should go into his Orchard, and find some withered Branches that were dead, and break them off, and graff in other Branches in the room thereof; doth this Act of his dissolve the Tree, or take it up by the Roots, (no sure) but it is in order to make the Tree more Fruitful. And for a full Corroboration of this, take our Saviour Chrisst's own evidence in *John* 15. 2. *Every branch in me that beareth not fruit, he taketh away: and every branch that beareth fruit, he purgeth it that it may bring forth more fruit.*

So that the everlasting Covenant is not Dissolved nor impaired in the least degree by the breaking off of some of the *Jews*, and taking in some of the Gentiles into it in their room.

11. Now Sir if you can find us out but one Text of Scripture in the whole Book of God that doth Corroborate your Position or contradict mine; then, but not until then you will do your

your busine(s, you must prove that w
believing *Jews*; those unfruitful Bra
broken off and cast out, that all t[
of the believing *Jews* which stood w
with them; and also that none but t[
lieving Gentiles were taken in, this
Sir, and do it if you can: for it must [
wise all your fine Spun Arguments wil
ground and be lost.

12. We find that the Infant Seed (
were included in the Covenant whic
with *Abraham*; as you see I have cle

Therefore if the Seed of the beli(
were cast out, and the Seed of 'bel
tiles not taken in; then the Covena[
be an everlasting Covenant, as God
is to Believers and their off-spring :
shall we believe (God) that cannot
H. C. judge ye?

13. I have observed that in all
Book I cannot find, that he hath been
as once to repeat the words of the cov
God made with *Abraham*, tho' he ha
ed, *Gen.* 17. 7. twice in Page 14.
very quintessence of the Covenant [
looks as if he were afraid there was th[
would have opened the peoples Eyes.
of that, he hath given the Covenant a
viz. The Covenant of peculiarity made wi
But this is the misery of these po(
People, any thing will down with
be but in favour of their Opinion;
noble *Berean* Spirit in them to [arc]
tures, to see whether these things [
and not to take all upon trust, as the

14. Wherefore in the 14th plac(
down God's Covenant, which he d

lbraham, as I have our Author's new-
it; And let us see how incongruous
'n. 17. 7. *And I will establish my cove-*
me and thee, and thy seed after thee,
rations, for an everlasting Covenant;
ito thee, and to thy seed after thee.
t may be, some will be so bold as to
is *Everlasting* imports no more, then
; as the *Mosaick* Dispensation did last:
iath nullified this vain Supposition,
ut of all doubt, in these Words,
, *He hath remembred his covenant for*
d which he commanded to a thousand

it a Thousand Generations between
God's making and declaring this Co-
Abraham, and the coming in of the
ow not: Nor one quarter so many

venant he made with *Abraham*, and
) *Isaac*, and confirmed the same unto
aw, and to *Israel* for an Everlasting
What think ye now, Sir, of your
peculiarity made with *Abraham* by
who, nor you neither? For if you
ht to have told us, and not to leave
int, as wise as you found us. But
t of peculiarity of yours, and God's
Covenant do not sound well together
ley make no Musick at all.
hy should you deal thus unfaithfully
:ople, as to hide those things from
:ep them in the dark, by your im-
Novelties in the room thereof! Is it
u had rather cover, and hide the
he People? then that your corrupt
most erroneous Explanations should
be

be detected, Would it not look very strange for a Minister of the Gospel in his Pulpit to name his Text, and never read the Words thereof? Which is just like the *Red-Letter* Guides: Even so you have done the same thing in effect; for you treated about the Covenant, and named the Chapter and Verse wherein it is contained, but you never read the Words.

18. But I find it is common for Men of your Opinion to bring in, and set up their own corrupt carnal Reason in opposition to the Wisdome and Grace of God, (as I have already hinted,) *viz.* By that unbelieving, but common Interrogation, namely, *What are young Infants capable of?* Which might be retorted, What are Adult Persons capable of, until some previous Act of the Spirit pass upon their Souls? When they are dead in Trespasses and Sins, it must be the omnipotent power of God's Grace, that must raise them from the Grave of a natural state into Spiritual Life, *Eph.* 2. 1. *And you hath he quickened who were dead in trespasses and sins.*

2. *What were young Children capable of at Eight Days old, under the Law?*

3. And Lastly, *What were those Children capable of, that entred into Covenant with the Lord in* Deut. 29. 9, 10, 11, 12, 13.?

I have Answered the two former Queries sufficiently already, therefore I will only Answer this latter, *Keep therefore the words of this covenant, and do them, that ye may prosper in all that ye do.*

Ye stand this day all of you before the Lord your God; your captains of your tribes, your elders, and your officers, with all the men of Israel,

Your little ones, your wives, and thy stranger that is in thy camp, from the hewer of thy wood, unto the drawer of thy water:

That

(93)

ouldest enter into covenant with the
and into his oath, which the Lord thy
h thee this day:

ay observe by the way, that these
ople before; for it is twice said,
d: But it may be queried, whether
enant distinct from that which God
braham? No; for the following
he contrary, in these Words,
establish thee to day for a people unto
at he may be unto thee a God, as he
thee, and as he hath sworn unto thy
aham, to Isaac, and to Jacob.
re been any People amongst them
Author pretends himself to be,
ve replyed, Our Children are not
r into Covenant for themselves, for
cannot speak: Well, but however
t, because God did command it:
hey do it, seeing they cannot do
Why, undoubtedly they did it by
Parents, or other Friends, did it
Vowing, and solemnly Ingaging,
rd, in Dedicating and Resigning
God by Covenant, that they would
in the Fear and Admonition of
Instruct them in all the Duties of
Relation they stood in to God, and
perswade them, when they were
ake hold of the Promise in the Co-
th for themselves, and to be often
in mind of it: This I humbly con-
Import of these little Childrens
the Lord, and making a Covenant

s as much a Duty incumbent upon
evers now, to bring their young
Children

solemnly dedicate their Children u[nto God,]
from whom they received them, no[t to keep them to]
God for them, as we ought to do f[or the encrease]
of our Cattle, but to resign them [up to him as their]
Lords by a perpetual Covenant in t[heir whole mainte-]
nance, and openly to own and ackn[owledge his]
Propriety in them, and his Soveraign[ty over them;]
Baptism hath an Analogy with Chri[st's Circumcision,]
which was his Baptism, wherein h[e was dedicated;]
so must all the Subjects be in Baptis[m.]

20. It is a solemn Ingagement b[y Parents]
before the Lord, to take all the [care that]
they can, to Train up their Childre[n in the Chri-]
stian Religion, to instruct them in [the Doctrine]
of Justification by the Righteousn[ess of Christ,]
through Faith, and the Doctrine of [Sanctification]
by his Word and Spirit, and to wat[ch over them,]
and pray for them, that they may li[ve soberly and]
godly Lives; and thus to train up a [Child, when]
he is young, he will not depart from [it when he]
is old. The Faith and Prayers of [Parents]
are very prevalent with God, for th[eir Children.]

And did Parents make more Cons[cience of per-]
forming this Duty, in discharging t[he Baptismal]
Obligation with a respect to their Ch[ildren, I am]
perswaded, we should soon see, tha[t God would]
put a difference between our Chil[dren, and the]
Children of those that are against In[fant-Baptism.]

But many Parents instead of dis[charging this]
Ingagement, do cocker their Child[ren]

care of them: Juſt like the Eſteridge, that lays her Eggs in the Sand, and never takes care what becomes of them. But, faith our Adverſaries, theſe Children may refuſe to ſtand to this Covenant, and nullifie all: So might Gods People have alledged in *Deut.* 29. For it is a great Queſtion whether All their Children ſtood to that Covenant or not; but if they did not, that might not have been their Parents Fault, but their own. But this is no Excuſe for Parents to neglect their Duty. Remember *Saul's* carnal Policy, and how dear it coſt him; he was for ſaving the beſt of the Cattel for Sacrifice, as he pretended: But do you all go and learn what that meaneth, which the Prophet told him, *Obedience is better than ſacrifice.*

The Remiſneſs of Pædobaptiſts do not at all Extenuate the Guilt of your contemning, and total neglecting that Ordinance to your Children, who are as vain as any other Profeſſors Children are; the negligence of the one, and the contemning by the other, may be Sins equivalent, and between theſe Two Extreams, there have been produced ſuch a debauched, degenerated, young Generation of Apoſtates, as there is at this Day, for which God is angry, and contending with us.

I do wonder that this Author ſhould have the confidence, and the ignorance, to fix upon *Rom.* 11. 19, 20, 21. to prove the Diſſolution of the Covenant of Peculiarity, as he calls it, made with *Abraham.* But this is to be obſerved, that he made uſe of no other Words in the Texts then theſe, *viz. The branches are broken off*, and runs away from the reſt of the Verſes, like one skared
out

out of his Wits, and never came at them again as you may see in *Page* 12. aforesaid.

Whereas the Covenant God made with *Abraham* was confirmed by his Oath unto *Isaac*, and to *Jacob*, for a Law, and to *Israel* for an Everlasting Covenant, and to all their Seed, which Covenant was from Everlasting Decretally, and to Everlasting Effectually, and can never be disanulled nor Repealed, because it was confirmed of God in Christ: There is the Center and Foundation of all, *Gal.* 3. 16, 17. *Psal.* 89. And that the Covenant, which God made with *Abraham*, is devolved upon us Gentiles, under the Dispensation of the Gospel, is as clear as the Sun, *Acts* 2. 39. *Gal.* 3. 8, 14. *Eph.* 3. 6. Wherefore he that is a True [Believer] [himself,] and all his [Children,] are as really in the same Covenant, as ever *Abraham* and his Seed were, and may plead all the Promises with God by Faith in Christ, for himself and his Children, that do belong to the Covenant, and all the Priviledges thereof, as ever *Abraham* for his Seed could do. What tho' we have not the Land of *Canaan?* Which was but a Temporal Blessing; yet we have that which is equivalent, *Matt.* 6. 33. *But seek ye first the kingdom of God, and his righteousness, and all these things shall be added unto you.*

And what these things are, you have in the 6 foregoing Verses, and in *Rom.* 8. 32. *He that spared not his own Son, but delivered him up for us all, how shall he not with him also freely give us all things?*

And the Apostle saith, *Godliness is profitable unto all things, having the promise of the life that now is, and of that which is to come.*

Is not here as much wrapt up in these Promises, as is contained in the Promise of the Land of
Canaan?

Canaan? And infinitely more; for many that did partake of the Blessings of the Terrene *Canaan* never did, nor never shall partake of the Heavenly *Canaan*; but none that ever did, or do partake of those Blessings aforesaid, shall ever miss of Heaven.

19. In the last place, That the Covenant which God made with *Abraham*, from which some of the Natural Branches were broken off, was never Dissolved nor Repealed, is undeniably evident from this, namely, That all the Jews, those Natural Branches, when it pleaseth God to convert them, will be graffed into their own *Olive-tree* again. How then is it possible that the Covenant can be Dissolved, or Repealed? See *Rom.* 11. 15, 24, 26. *For if the casting away of them be the reconciling of the world; what shall the receiving of them be, but life from the dead?*

For if thou wert cut out of the olive-tree which is wild by nature, and wert graffed contrary to nature into a good olive-tree; (This *olive-tree* which is wild by nature, was the First Covenant which God made with *Adam*; and the good *olive-tree* is the Covenant which God made with *Abraham*.) *how much more shall these which be the natural branches, be graffed into their own olive-tree.*

And so all Israel shall be saved: as it is written, There shall come out of Sion the deliverer, and shall turn away ungodliness from Jacob.

Thus you see the Covenant, which God made with *Abraham*, is Everlasting, and cannot be Dissolved, nor Repealed, because it stands fixed in the Oath and Faithfulness of God.

Now, Sir, I hope you have enough of the Dissolution of your Covenant of Peculiarity made with *Abraham*; and you are farther off (now)

from proselyting me to your Opinio[n]
for the more I Rake into it, the w
it ; therefore you shall never b[e]
to open my Eyes, as you arrogantl[y]
1. until you can see better your self,
of Scriptures, and not to take the
the Olive-tree, for the Roots thereo[f]
Physician cure thy self; first cast [out]
out of thine own Eye, and then [shalt thou see]
clearly to pluck out the Mote which
ther's Eye.

17. And Lastly, In Page 12. it
that the Church-State under the L[aw was]
carnal, as all their Ordinances we[re]
the Constitution of that Church w[as]
and so the Church-State also was p[laced on]
the Roots, as well as the Covenant
which was made with *Abraham*; and
Opinion are pleased to call it A [Legal Church]

In the first place to this I Answer,
of God under the *Mosaick* Law, was
Legal Church, though the Ordinan[ces and Cere-]
monies were, but Shadows and Ty[pes, yet the]
Spirit of God was dwelling in that
Christ was enjoyed under those Or[dinances]
(although) those Ordinances were m[ore dark]
under the Law than the Ordinance[s un-]
der the Gospel, yet the Church-Stat[e is Spiri-]
tual, and of the same Essence with
now, (that) was the Mother (Church)
and not the Synagogue of *Rome*, and
state was never broken nor hewn d[own till]
the Baptist, as I shall prove by and b[y out of the]
Mouth of *John the Baptist* himself.
Frame of the Church is more Refine[d under the]
Gospel than it was under the Law, bu[t]

State is the same still, and ever shall be : But our Authour saith, That the Church-State was only Carnal as their Ordinances were, and the Covenant in which the Church stands, is taken up by the Roots, and that all this was executed and perpetrated by *John the Baptist*, that he cut down the Church, and all the Members thereof, so that Infant Church-Membership was utterly cut off then, and yet he hath the confidence to deny that he intended Infants when he cited *John the Baptists* telling them, *That the Axe was laid to the Root of the Trees, and that they were to be hewn down, and cast into Eternal Fire*, in page 10.

These are their Positions, and my work is to disprove them, and also to prove the Church-State to be the same now under the Gospel, as it was under the Law.

1. And therefore I do in the first place positively declare that the State of the Church of Christ, is the very same now, as it was under the Law, and hath the same Attributes, and made of the same Ingredients, and hath the same Titles, and Lives upon the very same Food, and was a Baptized Church, and stood in the same Relation to God and Christ as the Gospel-Church doth now.

And if I can prove these five things clearly from Scripture, I hope no body will be so Impious as to deny the Truth on't.

1. I will begin with the Attributes of the Church of God under the Law, in *Exod.* 19. *Now therefore if you will obey my voice indeed, and keep my Covenant, then ye shall be a peculiar Treasure unto me, above all People, for all the Earth is mine.*

And ye shall be unto me a Kingdom of Priests, and an holy Nation, these are the words which thou shalt speak unto the Children of *Israel*, *Psal.*

135. 4. *For the Lord hath chosen Jacob unto himself, and Israel for his peculiar Treasure.*

Now 2. Compare these Attributes of the Church of God under the Law, with the Attributes of the Church of God under the Gospel, 1 *Pet.* 2. 9, 10. *But ye are a chosen generation, a royal Priesthood, an holy nation, a peculiar people, that ye should show forth the praises of him, who hath called you out of darkness into his marvellous light; which in time past were not a people, but are now the people of God, which had not obtained mercy, but now have obtained mercy.* These were the Gentile Churches, *Rev.* 1. 6. *And hath made us Kings and Priests unto God, and to his Father.* Thus you see the Attributes are the same now under the Gospel, as they were under the Law,

2. The Ingredients that the Church is made with now are the same.

1. Under the Law, *Exod.* 25. 31. *And thou shalt make a Candlestick of pure Gold, of beaten-work shall the Candlestick be made, his shafts and his branches, his bowls, his knops, and his flowers, shall be of the same*) that this is the Church and the Ordinances of God, will evidently appear by and by.

2. Under the Gospel, *Rev.* 1. 12. *And I turned to see the voice that spake with me, and being turned, I saw Seven Golden Candlesticks*: Thus you see the Ingredients are the same under the Gospel, as the Church under the Law was made of.

3. The Titles of the Church are the same.

1. The Titles under the Law are the same with those under the Gospel. *Zech.* 4. *And the Angel that talked with me, came again, and wakened me, as a man that is wakened out of his sleep, and said unto me, what seest thou, and I said, I have looked, and behold a candlestick all of Gold, with a bowl upon the top of it, and his seven lamps thereon, and seven*

pipes

pipes to *the seven lamps which were upon the top thereof;* and *two Olive-Trees by it, one upon the right side of the bowl, and the other upon the left side thereof:* Some Expositors interpret these two Olive-Trees to be meant of *Zerubbabel* and *Joshua*, the one as he was a Magistrate, and the other as a Priest, which I conceive represented Christ as King and Priest in the Church; and I will give you my reason for this my Conception, when I come to compare this with the Gospel-Church: *And I answered again, and said unto him, What be those two Olive-branches, which through the two Golden Pipes, empty the Golden Oil out of themselves.*

These two Golden Pipes, I humbly conceive is meant of the two Ordinances, *viz.* Of Circumcision and the Passeover under the Law, which were Typical of the Two Sacraments under the Gospel, the one of Baptisme, and the other of the Lords Supper: And the Seven Lamps I take to be the Church Officers, but principally Pastors and Teachers, as in *Zech.* 3. *Upon one stone shall be seven eyes.* This Stone or Rock is the Church, and the seven Eyes are the same with the seven Lamps; for the Ministers are in a sence the Peoples Eyes, and agree with the same number of Stars in the Gospel-Church, which are also for Light to the People; and the Branches are all the Members of the Church, who are called Branches, in *John* 15. 1, 2. *Rom.* 11. 17. And they may be called Two upon this account, *viz.* To represent, both the Adult and Infant Members thereof, and he answered me, *and said, Knowest thou not what these be, and I said, no my Lord: Then said he, these are the two anointed ones which stand by the Lord of the whole Earth.*

of *Zerubbabel* and *Joshua*, but Antitypical, for I humbly conceive as I said before, They represent Christ as King and Priest in the Church, which Two Offices especially are invaded by Antichrist, who hath assumed the said Offices himself, 2 *Thes.* 2. 4, 5. Against which Usurpation lay the Witnesses great Work and Business in *Rev.* 11. to bear their Testimony; and these Two Candlesticks here in this Chapter, I take to be Prophetically spoken of the Two Nations, *viz.* Jews and Gentiles, in Church Order at their Conversion, after the Destruction of Antichrist.

And my Reason for it is this, Because where the Gentiles were spoken of, as formed into Church Order, we find more than two; and where God treated with his People under the Law, in forming them into Church Order, we find but one, *Exod.* 25. 31.

Now here the Scripture Interprets what these Golden Candlesticks are, in *Rev.* 1. 12, 20. *And I turned to see the voice that spake with me, and being turned, I saw seven Golden Candlesticks. The Mystery of the Seven Stars which thou sawest in my right hand, and the seven Golden Candlesticks; the seven stars are the seven Angels of the seven Churches;* These are the Pastors and Teachers, &c. of the Churches, which are represented by seven Lamps, and seven Eyes, for they are the Eyes of the People called Seers in Scripture; *Exod.* 25. *And thou shalt make the seven lamps thereof, and they shall light the lamps thereof, that they may give light over against it,* as the seven Stars are lights in the Church, so were the seven lamps: and Gospel-Ministers and Godly-People are compared

pared to Light in Scripture : *Let your light so shine before men*, &c.

4. The Church of God under the *Mosaick* Law lived upon the same Spiritual Food as the Church of Christ doth now under the Gospel; only the Dishes are not the same, but are changed, *viz.* the Ordinances (though of the same use) the Golden Pipes that convey the Golden Oil of God's Grace, and empty themselves into the Branches or Vessels of Mercy, *viz.* into the Souls of all the Elect Church-Members that are in Christ, and that they lived upon the same Spiritual Food is an undenyable Truth, as you may see, 1 *Cor.* 10. *Moreover Brethren, I would not that ye should be ignorant how that all our Fathers were under the cloud, and all passed through the Sea, and did all eat the same spiritual meat, and did all drink the same spiritual drink, for they drank of that spiritual Rock that followed them, and that Rock was Christ*: Mind ye, They all lived and fed upon Christ by Faith in that day, and so do all true Believers now.

5. And lastly, The Church of God under the Law was a baptized Church; they were all baptized, Men, Women, and Children; and there can be no true Church but what is so now; and the Apostle would not have Christians to be ignorant of it now, 1 *Cor.* 10. 1, 2. *Moreover Brethren, I would not that ye should be ignorant how that all our Fathers were under the cloud, and all passed through the Sea; and were all baptized unto Moses in the cloud and in the Sea*: Here is a Church baptized by the immediate hand of God, and not one of them Dipped nor Ducked over Head and Ears: O all ye *Anabaptists* that call for an Example for the baptizing the Infant-Seed of Believers, If that of baptizing of whole Housholds, nor of *John the Baptist* baptizing all the *Jews* that came unto him:

him, Young and Old will not do: Behold here is a greater than the Example of all thefe, For here God himfelf hath given us an Example for the baptizing all the Children of Chriftian Parents, whether they may prove to be Believers or not, when they come to be Grown Perfons, which is a fecret thing, and belongeth to God: But we are not to Reprobate our own Children, but to hope well of them, and to take care to Educate them in the fear of the Lord, and inftruct them in the Principles of the Chriftian Religion, and to be much in praying and believing for them, though I know our Faith and Prayer cannot merit ought at the hands of God for them, no more than the Faith and Prayer, and Anointing of the Sick with Oil can in *James* 5. 14, 15. Though our Prayers are not Meritorious, yet you fee they are Efficacious.

Thus I have clearly proved, That the Church of Chrift under the Law, was the very fame that now is under the Gofpel, only fhe hath changed her *Ornaments*, and the Apoftle gave the chief Officers of the Church under the Law, the Right Hand of Fellowfhip in that Reverend Relative Title he gave them, in which he claimed the Relation of a Father to a Son: And you may fee that the Church of God under the Law was the fame as is now under the Difpenfation of the Gofpel, by Chrifts Deed of conveyance in which he made it over to the *Gentiles* and their Heirs, which were called in, and grafted into the *Olive-Tree*, among the *Jews* and their Children that ftood under the new Difpenfation: Pray read the Deed, for look ye here it is in *Matth.* 21. 4. *Therefore I fay unto you, the kingdom of God fhall be taken from you*: And what then, Did Chrift deftroy stroy it? No; But it was given to a Nation bringing forth the Fruits thereof. What do you think on't now? Was this a carnal Church? And yet you see those Members of it were carnal, or Christ would never have excommunicated them, or unchurch'd them. What think ye was the Church destroyed by this Act of Christ's or not? For if this did not do it, then it is standing still to this Day, and ever will.

2. In the second place a little by way of Amplification; First, Let us observe strictly what can be gathered from the Words of *John* the Baptist, whereby any manner of Ground or Reason there is to be laid hold on, to fix this Solution of our Author's upon, *viz*. That *John* the Baptist did Abolish the Church-State, and took up the Covenant by the Roots, and so for ever excluded the Infant Seed of Believers Church-Membership.

3. Pray let us hear what *John* himself saith in *Matth.* 3. 10. *And now also the ax is laid unto the root of the trees: therefore every tree which bringeth not forth good fruit is hewen down, and cast into the fire.* But our Author hath added *eternal fire*, in Page 53. (*Mat.* 7. 19.) But pray why should Children be included in this Text of Scripture? when you will not allow them to be included in *Mark* 16. where it is said, *He that believeth and is baptized, shall be saved, but he that believeth not, shall be damned.* [*Every tree,*] and [*he that believeth not:*] Are not Children as much included in one, as in the other, and that by your own Argument too? but you will by no means allow of the Latter, as in Page 5. But this by the way,

John the Baptist preached Repentance, and Holiness of Life unto them, and withal dehorted

them

them from resting upon their external Priviledges, in saying, *We have, Abraham to our Father:* And from this they conclude, that the Church-State was cut down. But alas! If this was to cut down the Church, it was so cut down many Hundreds of Years before, by the Prophet *Jeremiah*, and was not left for *John* to do (then;) For they were not to live wickedly before, nor rest in their External Priviledges any more, than they were then, or now; for God did not Erect his Church to Indulge Wickedness, which must be the consequence, if the Church was a carnal Church; for Carnality and Spirituality are opposite. Pray see for the confutation of this carnal Epithet this Man hath given the Church of God, *Jer.* 7. 4. *Trust ye not in lying words, saying, The temple of the Lord, the temple of the Lord,* &c.

Here the Prophet dehorts them from resting in external Priviledges, as much as ever *John* did, if not more; for then he proceeds to rip up their carnal Wickedness, and lays the Threatnings, and also the Executions done by God before them, in these Verses following, 8, 9, 10, 11, 12.

Behold, ye trust in lying words, that cannot profit.

Will ye steal, murder, and commit adultery, and swear falsly, and burn incense unto Baal, and walk after other gods whom ye know not;

And come and stand before me in this house, which is called by my name, and say, We are delivered to do all these abominations?

Is this house, which is called by my name, become a den of robbers in your eyes? behold, even I have seen it, saith the Lord.

Here you see the Church was called by God's Name, and our Author calls it a carnal Church; now God is not a carnal God, therefore the
Church

Church is not a carnal Church; for God is a Spirit, and they that worship him must worship him in Spirit and in Truth: The Church in it self was Spiritual.

But the Prophet in Verse 12. directs them where to go, to see what Execution God had done upon carnal Professors, and Church-members that were wicked.

But go ye now unto my place which was in Shiloh, where I set my name at the first, (that was, where there was a Church,) *and see what I did to it, for the wickedness of my people Israel.*

This was far more like the cutting down the Church State, than that of *John* the Baptist's preaching Repentance to the Pharisees and Sadducees: For the Axe was not only laid to the Root of the Trees, but there were many Thousands of them cut down, and yet the Axe never touched the Church-State.

3. If to preach Repentance, and to apply the Threatnings unto the Impenitent, be to destroy the Church of Christ, or to rest in External Priviledges, then is the Church in great danger, if not destroyed, by many Sermons that are preached. Indeed, God hath removed his Church from one Nation, or People, to another under the Gospel; but the Church abideth firm: The Gates of Hell shall never prevail against it. Our Saviour told the Scribes, Pharisees, and Hypocrites, That the Kingdome of Heaven, which was the Church, should be taken from them, and given to a Nation, bringing forth the Fruits thereof: These were the Gentiles:

If a King betrusts a Rich Jewel with one of his Subjects, and finds that he abuses his Favour, which causeth him to take it from him, and put it into the Hands of another; Doth he thereby destroy yet People may sin so as to provoke God to unchurch them, as God did those unbelieving Jews, namely, some of the Natural Branches, and several Churches under the Gospel Dispensation.

4. But seeing they have taken up this Text of *John* the Baptist's, to destroy the Church by, let us see whether *John* will own it, or whether he can be any way chargeable with this which they have Fathered upon him; for I dare not trust them in what they say in this Controversie, because I find some of them matter not what they say themselves, nor what they make others say, that are not in being to speak for themselves, and it may be we may find that this Author hath wronged *John* the Baptist also, and therefore let us hear what the Scripture saith; and compare Scripture with Scripture.

Mat. 3. *And now also the ax is laid unto the root of the trees,*] Mind, It is said Trees in the plural, which could not be meant of the Church; for had it intended the Church under the Law, it must have been Tree in the singular; but this must respect Rotten Members, or Branches, as they are called in *John* 15. 2. *Rom.* 11. Now could this be meant of that one Golden Candlestick? No sure! It is impossible for the Reasons aforesaid. But to proceed,

5. In the fifth place pray mind the 11. and 12. Verses of *Mat.* 3. *I indeed baptize you with water unto repentance; but he that cometh after me, is mightier than I, whose shoes I am not worthy to bear: he shall baptize you with the holy Ghost, and with fire.*

Whose

Whose fan is in his hand, and he will throughly purge his floor, and gather his wheat into the garner: but he will burn up the chaff with unquenchable fire.

Doth a Farmer destroy his Barn, or so much as hurt the Floor of it, when he takes a great Heap of Corn and Chaff, that lieth together, one among another, on the Floor, and winnows the Corn, and fans away the Chaff? Surely no: For this is that which *John* alludes unto, to declare that Christ was coming to purge and refine the Church; but not to destroy it; and to break off those superfluous, barren Branches; but not to pluck it up by the Roots; *John* 15. 1. *I am the true vine, and my Father is the husbandman.*

Verse 2. *Every branch in me that beareth not fruit, he taketh away: and every branch that beareth fruit, he purgeth it, that it may bring forth more fruit.*

6. Here you see *John* the Baptist came before Christ with the Axe of God's Threatning, against those unfruitful Branches, namely, particular Church-Members, in case they did not repent; and our Saviour Christ came after with his Fan in his Hand, and Executed the Threatning, by blowing the chaffy Hypocrites away out of his Floor, the Church: He did not blow the Church from them; but he fanned them out of the Church, but the Church remained still, fixed and firm. The Church-State is like God himself, unchangeable, *Eph.* 2. 19. *Now therefore ye are no more strangers and forreiners, but fellow-citizens with the saints, and of the houshold of God;*

Verse 20. *And are built upon the foundation of the apostles and prophets, Jesus Christ himself being the chief corner-stone;*

Verse 21. *In whom all the building fitly framed together, groweth unto an holy temple in the Lord;*

Verse 22. *In whom you also are builded together for an habitation of God through the Spirit.*

Here the Holy Ghost hath joined the old Dispensation of the Church under the Law to the new Dispensation of the Church under the Gospel, and also joined the Jews and Gentiles together.

(1.) You may observe, They are all Fellow-citizens, which imports but one City; for if they had been of two distinct Cities, then they could not be Fellow-citizens.

(2.) They are all of one and the same Family, *viz.* The Houshold of God.

(3.) They are built upon the same Foundation, and therefore the Prophets are mentioned as well as the Apostles, which doth clearly Evince the Truth of it.

(4.) Christ is the chief Corner-stone in all the Building.

(5.) It is a most compact Building, fitly framed together.

(6.) And Lastly, It is a Habitation for God. Now is the Law of Man so severe against those that destroy a Man's House? What must they be guilty of, that destroy the House of God! As all they do that Assert, That the Church under the Law was but a carnal, legal Church, and that it was destroyed at the coming in of the Gospel.

Christ did not destroy the Church with his Fan, but purged it: He did not blow away one Grain of the Wheat, *viz.* of the believing *Hebrews*, nor their children; (No;) but they all remained Church-Members, under the Gospel: For it were these the Apostle writ the *Epistle of the Hebrews* unto; and the Gentiles, which also believed, were united unto Christ in Hhurch order, and they and their children were graffed into the same Olive-tree with the believing *Hebrews*. Rom. 11. 17. Thus

Thus I have clearly proved that there is no more in this Text in *Mat.* 3. to prove the Destruction of the Church State, at the coming in of the Gospel, than there is in *Rom.* 11. 19, 20, 21. to prove that the Covenant, which God made with *Abraham*, was taken up by the Root:

But it doth appear, That those that do Assert this aforesaid of *John* the Baptist do miserably abuse and slander him, in making him the Executioner of this cruel piece of Barbarity, viz. to cut down and destroy God's House and Habitation, *Eph.* 2. 22. and that he cut off all the Infant Seed of Believers. If *John* the Baptist was upon Earth, he would give the Anabaptists but little Thanks for their thus calumniating him; for *John* [never] so much as lifted up his Axe against the Church State, but the Axe was brought to lop off the unfruitful dead Branches, viz. Hypocrites and Formalists; and that was for the preservation of the Church, and not for the Destruction of it; for the Church is the same Church still, only she hath changed her Attire; she hath put on her Beautiful Gospel Ornaments, and changed her Houshold-stuff, which was then grown out of fashion; but the Building you see, was the same, *Eph.* 2. 19, 20, 21. And the Provision is the same without any variation or alteration; they lived by Faith then, and so they do now, 1 *Cor.* 10. 2, 3, 4. It is just as if a Married Wife should put off her old Cloathes, and put on a new Rich Suit of Apparel of her Husband's providing? Doth this destroy the Woman, or the Relation she stands in to her Husband and Children? No; nor theirs to her neither; but they stand in the same Relation one to another, as they did when she had on her old Cloaths: Why, even so it is between Christ and his Church, *Isa.* 54. 5.

For

For thy maker is thine husband, (the Lord of hosts is his name;) and thy redeemer the holy One of Israel, the God of the whole earth shall he be called.

Compare with Rev. 19. 7. *Let us be glad and rejoice, and give honour to him: for the marriage of the Lamb is come, and his wife hath made herself ready;* Rev. 21. 9, 10.

Here it may be observed, that the Church under the Law was Married to Christ, and Christ did not give her a Bill of Divorcement by the coming in of the Gospel, and Christ never had but one Wife.

Thus, under God I have proved the Church of Christ to be the same, and her Members of the same Sects and Ages now, as they were under the Law, and I have also utterly confuted all the Allegations and Arguments which the Adversaries of this *Great Truth* have, or ever will be capable to bring against it, and they are their own Witnesses, that they are no Church of God; for if the Gospel-church now is the same, as that was under the Law, and if theirs be not built by Faith on that Foundation, then they are no Church: But they affirm, that the old Church-State was destroyed; *Ergo*, they are no Church; and by that Principle of denying Infant Church-Membership, they can be but a Demy Church at best; and what the difference is, between a Demy Church, and no Church, I will appeal to the Reader for Judgment: For as good never a whit, as never the better; for in excluding their children, which are at least the one half of the Church, they exclude themselves also; for Christ saith, *Suffer little children, and forbid them not to come unto me, for of such is the kingdom of God,* Mark 10. That this is spoken of the Church is clear from this, because it is the very same Epithet

thet that is given to the Church in Chrift's Deed of conveyance to the Gentiles, *Matth.* 21. 43. *Therefore say I unto you, The kingdom of God shall be taken from you, and given to a nation bringing forth the fruits thereof.*

3. As they deprive their children of their Right, fo they rob the Church of the half of her Treafure, and thereby rob God of his Honour; for the Members of a Church are the peculiar Treafure of the Church, *Pfal.* 135. 4. Therefore the very Opinion of Anabaptifm is a moft Sacrilegious Opinion.

Thus I have given you one Broad-fide more, by which I have brought your whole Opinion by the Lee, and all the Carpenters and Calkers in the Nation cannot fave it from finking, and all your Florid, Specious, Syllogiftical Arguments are flain; there is not one of them left alive to carry Tydings.

And I have clearly proved, Elect dying Infants have Habitual Faith, and that the Covenant God made with *Abraham* was never diffolved, nor taken up by the Roots, and that *Jerufalem*, (the Church,) which is the Mother of us all, hath all her children about her, and that the Church of Chrift was never cut down, nor the Infant Seed of Believers cut off from being Church-Members; but they all ftand fixed in the Covenant now as much as ever they did under the Law. And I obferve, they never affign what the Sin was which thofe young Babes committed, that provoked God to deal fo feverely with them, as to caft them out of Covenant. And I have clearly Vindicated my Book, and cleared it from that *Foul Afperfion* of being *A Counterfeit*, and alfo from fetting my felf in a Pofture of War againft God : But I
confefs

confess you do make a God of your Opinion, and so you may justly say, that I set my self in a Posture of War against that God; And I have overcome him [too.]

And according to my promise, I have buried your *Dead Answer* to my Book: And my Advice unto you is, That you would humble your self before the Lord, for all the Abominations that you have set forth to the World, in your two most *Erroneous* Books, and make a publick Recantation of them all, and your Opinion to boot, and you will soon find the comfort and the benefit of it: for there is no Man so perfect, but that he is lyable to be Tempted and Tainted with Errours, and there is no Man too Great to stoop to Truth. Some that were as long of this Opinion as our Author, and as good Men every whit, (no undervaluing to him,) did bless God for this Book of mine, which they have so vilified: You ought not to despise the Meanness of the Instrument; that was none of your Practice before you came so well acquainted with the Two Universities, as to know what they are capable to Judge or Determine, as in *Page* 3. Though the Means or Instrument be never so mean and despicable, that God is pleased to make use of, yet despise not the Day of small Things. Now all that I will farther say to you at this time (though I could have said more) shall be this, Either comply with the Truths of God that is in this Book, or confute them if you can, by giving a clear Answer, either to all of it, or any part of it, and do not pretend to Answer it, as you did my last, when there is not one Thing Answered of the whole Book, as I will appeal to any judicious Person, and discharge your self from all those Things

which

which I have charged you with, for the Press is open for you as well as for me.

II.

Here are some Remarks upon some strange Doctrines I met with in a late Book, Written by Mr. Benjamin Keach., Intituled, The Axe laid to the Root, or one Blow more at the Foundation of Infants Baptism, and Church-Membership.

First, I will begin with *Page* 17. where he confidently Asserts, That God made two Covenants with *Abraham*, and chargeth them with blindness, that cannot see them in these Words, viz.

You must not reckon from Abraham, but from Christ: He must be blind that can't discern from hence, that there were two Covenants made with Abraham.

Pray mind, This Man consequentially doth reckon *Abraham* of greater Antiquity than Christ, even as the Jews did, who said unto them, *Verily, verily, I say unto you, Before Abraham was I am.*

1. Here it is to be observed, that he hath positively asserted, that God made two Covenants with *Abraham*, and saith, They must be blind that can't discern them.

But to prevent their seeing the contrary; in page 16, where he quoted *Gen.* 17. 9, 10. he left out and gave the 7th. *verse* the slip, wherein is contained the Tenour and the very Essential part of the Covenant, and goes on with his Theme
to

to prove his Two Covenants by, from the aforesaid Three Verses, but the words of the Seventh verse are these, *And I will Establish my Covenant between me and thee, and thy seed after thee, in their generations, for an Everlasting Covenant, to be a God unto thee, and to thy seed after thee*: And hear what *David* witnesses, *Psalm* 105. *He hath remembred his Covenant for ever, the word which he commanded to a thousand generations, which Covenant he made with Abraham, and his oath unto Isaac; and confirmed the same unto Jacob for a law, and unto Israel for an everlasting Covenant*. Who are blindest, He that can see Two Covenants made by God with *Abraham*, or they which can see but one; and that still remains in full Force and Vertue, and was never Dissolved nor Repealed as I have already sufficiently proved. Again,

2. In *page* 19, he hath quoted *Gen.* 17. 7, 8. and 11. *verses*, and left out the word, *An everlasting covenant*.

3. In page 21, he quotes *Gen.* 17. 9, 10, 11 but neither in these three quotations, nor in all his Discourse in his Book hath he so much as named that which is the very quintessence of the Covenant God made with *Abraham* to give it that Title which the Wisdom of God saw good to give it, namely, *an Everlasting Covenant*; this is like Mr. *H. C.* that never mentioned it as I ever could find in both his Books.

The Devil left out part of a Scripture once to tempt our Saviour Christ with, but in my weak Judgment this Authour hath done it three times successively to maintain this *Error* by, and I am jealous it was done willfully, the better to beguile and deceive poor Ignorant bigotted Souls, that take all upon Trust, and walk by an Implicit Faith.

He ought to have laid down the Covenant fairly, as it lies in the Text, and not to lead them blindfold, and say they are blind that can't see two Covenants God made with *Abraham*, when God hath said in *Gen.* 17. 7.' *And I will establish my Covenant between me and thee, and thy seed after thee, in their generations for an Everlasting Covenant to be a God unto thee, and to thy seed after thee.* Now if God had made Two Covenants with *Abraham*, it would have been thus said, *And I will establish my Covenants between me and thee, and thy seed after thee for Everlasting Covenants*; And not *an Everlasting Covenant* in the singular: But yet that would not have done it, unless the word [Everlasting] had been left out, for that spoils his design, and therefore he hath craftily chosen rather not to mention the word *Everlasting* at all. But,

2. ' Saith he, In *page* 18, some will still ob-
' ject, That though this which I have said be
' granted, that there were two Covenants made
' with *Abraham*, yet say they Circumcision was
' a Gospel-Covenant, or did appertain to the
' Covenant of Grace.

This is a subtle way indeed of begging the Question, but they must be very blind indeed that will grant this to be true that you say, That there were Two Covenants made by God with *Abraham* and his Seed, in *Gen.* 17. 7, 8, 9, 10, 11, 13. Pray observe what an Absurdity attends this Position: For then there would have been Three Covenants in being at once, Two Covenants of Works, and one of Grace; for if God made Two Covenants with *Abraham*, one of them must be of Works; for it is Non-sense to say they were both of Grace, or both of Works: For God to have Two differing Covenants of Works in
being

being at once, would be very ſtrange, and aſ ſtrange to have Two differing Covenants of Grace in being at one and the ſame time.

God made two Covenants with *Adam* indeed, but they were ſucceſſively one after another.

1. God made a Covenant of Works with him, *Gen.* 1. 16, 17. which Covenant our firſt Parents broke, and ſo it remains.

2. After they had broken that, God made a new one with them, namely, the Covenant of Grace, in *Gen.* 3. 15. And theſe two Covenants have contained all the Seed of *Adam* and all the Seed of *Abraham*, both under the Law, and under the Goſpel, and ever will; and they will be in thoſe Two Covenants to all Eternity, all that die in the Covenant of Grace ſhall be ſaved, and all that die in the Covenant of Works ſhall be Damned; for the one dyeth in the Lord, *Rev.* 13. 14, and the other dyeth in his Sins, *John* 8. 24.

Here you ſee I have proved that there is but Two Covenants, and the one belongeth to them that go to Heaven, and the other to them that goe to Hell. Now if there were another, then that did belong to them that goe to Purgatory. That there is an outſide and an inſide in the Everlaſting Covenant which God made with *Abraham*, I readily grant, or an outward Court and an inner Court, and but one Covenant ſtill as there is in the Church or Temple of God, *Rev.* 11. But none ſhall be ſaved, but them which are in the Inner Court, either of the Covenant, or Church, which is Chriſt's Myſtical Body; for there are Dead Members, Outward-Court-Worſhippers in that *John* 15. 1, 2. *I am the true vine, and my Father is the huſbandman. Every*

branch

hat beareth not fruit, he taketh away,
the Church.) Now I will bring you
ture to prove *Abrahams* Covenant to
me Nature; That there were two
ches in that *Rom.* 11. 17. *And if
nches be broken off,* &c.
21. ' Pray obſerve in the Old Co-
nts were Members, who did not
into that Covenant, and made
f that Legal Church; know the

ntions but one Covenant, and doth
that young Infants were in that
ſo that he hath confuted himſelf;
or any one of their Opinion prove
that ever God did caſt young Infants
e Covenant again: He hath deſtroy-
ovenants by thus contradicting him-
nder his Circumſtances need to have
ry.
e cometh with this Salvo, ' That
dditional Covenant, the New Cove-
te, *I will*, and *they ſhall*, that was a
of Works, this of Grace, &c.
all know me, from the leaſt, to the
ot an Infant then be ſure is in it as
f the Goſpel-Church, they are now
Repent, to Believe, to bring forth
for Repentance.
Vere not Faith and Repentance re-
the Legal Diſpenſation, as well as
oſpel, and was not Holyneſs and a
with God required then as much as
not as contrary to the Holy Nature
ch then as now? What is God fallen
only now under the Goſpel? But
, *That he would by no means acquit*
the

the guilty; and *Abraham believed in God, and it was accounted to him for righteousness: Enoch walked with God by Faith*: And *David repented*: Sin was no more tolerable under the Law, than it is under the Gospel: And how many times do we read of Gods punishing his People under the Law for Sin Was there ever such strange stuff as this imposed upon People? As if Sin was not as hateful to God under the Law as it is to him, now under the Gospel, you make God changeable, you make him to be that at one time, which he is not at another: Pray what Conditions are young Infants capable of performing personally, now under the Gospel, more than young Children were at Eight days old under the Law, that dyed in their Infancy; but notwithstanding Relatively they can in Christ, who of God is made unto all the Elect Wisdom and Righteousness, and Sanctification and Redemption; *For as in Adam all the Elect died, so in Christ they shall all be made alive*: What though Children cannot perform those Conditions personally of themselves, if Christ doth it for them; Is it not as well, nay, is it not infinitely better? And if an Adult Person cannot be saved without performing these conditions personally by vertue of Maturity of years, then, it is not a Covenant of Grace, but of Works: Now suppose a Man oweth a Thousand Pounds, and had not a penny to pay it with, yet if he hath a Rich Friend that will pay it for him, is not the Debt as well paid, and the Creditor as well satisfied as if he had paid it himself, or laid in Prison till he had. Christ hath done all for us and in us, as I have already sufficiently demonstrated, 1 *Pet.* 2. 24. *Who his own self bare our sins in his own body on the Tree, that we being dead to sin, should live unto Righteousness, by whose stripes ye were healed.*

1 *John*

And ye know that he was manifested
r sins, and in him is no sin. Acts 5.
God exalted with his right hand, to
d a Saviour, to give Repentance to
iveness of sin: He was made a Man
d brought into acquaintance with
roduct of Gods Eternal Love: For
r himself, no: *For in him was no*
our griefs, and carried our sorrows;
unded for our transgressions, he was
iniquities, the chastisement of our
n him, and with his stripes we are
l was made an offering for sin: Here
s of the Covenant of Grace lay upon
forme, and he hath done it, for
this done, for Adult Elected Persons
ect Dying Infants no share in these
f Christ, no; According to this
rtion they have not, because they
me these previous qualifications,
tural Tendency of his position: But
manner of Scripture that gives the
ace to this (I had almost said) popish
t I do positively declare, that Elect
are as capable every whit of recei-
its of the Conditions which Christ
rmed, as any Adult Person can be
eing it is brought about, and ap-
powerful Operation of the Holy
, both Old and Young, that belong
a of Grace: But besides, such In-
did sin against those Conditions
ir own Persons, though Originally
y they have.
a view of the Conditions that God
under the Gospel, to qualifie Per-
oung and Old, for Life and Salva-

F   tion,

tion, and compare them with the Conditions that were under the Law, and let us see if there be any difference.

Rom. 10. 20. *But Esaias is very bold, and saith, I was found of them that sought me not; I was made manifest unto them that asked not after me.* Isa. 65. 1.

Here you see what the Conditions were under the Law, and are now the same under the Gospel, and the Apostle hath brought them down to the Gospel, and joined them together.

Eph. 2. 12, 13. *That at that time ye were without Christ, being aliens from the common-wealth of Israel, and strangers from the covenants of promise, having no hope, and without God in the world:*

But now in Christ Jesus, ye who sometimes were far off, are made nigh by the blood of Christ.

Ezek. 16. 6. *And when I passed by thee, and saw thee polluted in thine own blood, I said unto thee when thou wast in thy blood, Live,* &c.

And when I passed by thee, and looked upon thee, behold, thy time was the time of love.

Now where are these previous Qualifications to be found, for the Performance of these Conditions? It may be you will say, That is the Conditions in *Phil.* 2. where it is said, *Work out your own salvation with fear and trembling.* Why, this is a Condition it is true, or a command to a Duty, but mind how these Conditions are to be performed, or this Command obeyed, Verse 13. *For it is God which worketh in you, both to will and to do of his good pleasure.* Here you see it is God that doth it for them; and can't God do it for a Child, that hath no Actual Sin to oppose him? Now see how this agrees with the Old Testament, *Isa.* 26. 12. *Lord, thou wilt ordain peace for us: for thou also hast wrought all our works in us.*

Here

Here you see how compatible these Scriptures are, *John* 7. 37. *In the last day, that great day of the feast, Jesus stood and cried, saying, If any man thirst, let him come unto me, and drink.*

Isa. 55. 1. *Ho, every one that thirsteth, come ye to the waters, and he that hath no money; come ye, buy and eat, yea, come, buy wine and milk without money, and without price.*

But you will say, Is not here a Condition, *viz.* They must [come?] Indeed I must confess, it is a Condition; (but a very easie one, we should think;) for they are to have every thing freely, for nothing but fetching, and can't they do that? No. But as easie a Condition as you think it is, if God should leave us to perform it of our selves, we should never do it; for Christ saith, *None can come to me except the Father, which sent me, draw them:* And it is God that maketh them willing; but when? Why, in the Day of his Power, that is at his time, and by what Means he pleaseth.

2. When Christ was lifted up, that is, when he was crucified, he drew all Men to him: That was vertually and meritoriously by his Death and Sufferings: For by vertue of the Transactions of Christ upon the Cross, all the Elect of God, both Old and Young, sooner or later, are drawn to close with Christ. And that Children can thus come to Christ by vertue of his Crucifiction, is beyond all doubt, if you will believe Christ himself, *Matth.* 19. 14. *But Jesus said, Suffer little children, and forbid them not to come unto me: for of such is the kingdom of heaven.*

Thus I hope you are satisfied how Elect dying Infants do perform these Conditions, namely, Faith and Repentance; for you see it is Christ that doth all for them, and in them, Aye, and for the Adult too; for of our selves we can do

F 2   nothing;

nothing; but we can do all things through Chrift that ftrengthneth us. And you fee that as the Covenant is the fame now, as it was under the Law, fo are the Conditions thereof, which alone is a fufficient Evidence that the Covenant is the fame, and is not diffolved, nor taken up by the Roots, as fome Men dream it is.

All the Conditions is by Faith on a crucified Saviour, which is ever accompanied with Evangelical Repentance, and Godly Sorrow for fin which are beft performed by beholding of a crucified Saviour, to fee him in his bloody Agony in the Garden fweating great Drops of Blood, to behold him fuffering under the Burden of our fins, and under the Burden of his Fathers wrath to fee his Righteous Soul made an Offering for fin, and to fee his finlefs Body offered up a Sacrifice upon the Crofs, and to fee him under the Burden of the Wrath and Malice of Blood-thirfty Men, to fee him that was, and is, and is to come the greateft Bleffing made a Curfe for fin, to fee his Glorious Body faft nailed to the Crofs through his Hands and Feet, hanging thereby with the weight of his Body, and to fee him crowned with the Curfe of the Earth, and to fee his Bleffed Side gufhing out with Blood and Water, and to hear him crying out, in the Anguifh of his Sufferings *My God, my God, why haft thou forfaken me?* And to fee his Enemies give him that bitter Portion of Vinegar and Gall to drink: Oh! what amazing Love was this! And all this he did and fuffered for the Elects fake, both Old and Young; therefore thus to look upon him whom we have pierced and mourn, is true Evangelical Repentance, to look upon our own fins with abhorrence, and to admire and praife God for his wonderful Redeeming Love, and Chrift commands us to look upon
him

him and be faved; and this muft be effected by the mighty powerful Influence of the Holy Spirit dwelling in us, and anointing of us; fo that all the whole Building of the Salvation of all God's Elect, both Young and Old, from the Foundation to the Top-ftone, is all of Free Grace.

4. In Page 25. faith our Author, 'Perhaps 'fome may Object, *If Infants as fuch, were not* 'included *in the Covenant of Grace God made with* '*Abraham, how can dying Infants be faved?*

'1. I Anfwer, Muft Infants of Believers be 'comprehended in that Covenant God made 'with *Abraham?* Or elfe, cannot any Dying In-'fants be faved? How then were any faved before '*Abraham's* Days, or before that Covenant was 'made with him.

Pray mark, He hath Anfwered this Objection as if there had been no Covenant of Grace before the time that God did declare, and make that Covenant with *Abraham*; as if there had not been Grace fufficient in the Covenant which God made with *Adam* after the Fall, to fave Elect dying Infants before *Abraham's* time; for all the Elect, both young and Old, from *Adam* to *Abraham*, and from *Abraham* to the End of the World, were, are, and fhall be faved in the Covenant of Grace, by Faith in our Lord Jefus Chrift. Remember what Chrift himfelf faith, *Before Abraham was I am.*

The Covenant which God made with *Adam* after the Fall, and Ratified it under a new Difpenfation with *Abraham*, was one and the fame Covenant, which was the Fruit and Effects of the Covenant of Redemption between God the Father and Jefus Chrift, from all Eternity; which God was pleafed then to declare, and make particularly, to *Abraham* and his Family, and to all his

his Seed and Off-spring, both Jews and also the Gentiles, that were not of his Natural Seed, as he was a Type of Christ, *Gal.* 3. 14, 16, 17. *That the blessing of Abraham might come on the Gentiles through Jesus Christ; that we might receive of the spirit through faith.*

Now to Abraham and his seed were the promises made. He saith not ; And to seeds, as of many ; but as of one, And to thy seed, which is Christ.

This I humbly conceive, respects Christ as Mediator, who as Man proceeded from the Loyns of *Abraham*, according to the Flesh. Pray mind *Matth.* 1. 1. *The book of the generation of Jesus Christ, the son of David, the son of Abraham.*

Gal. 3. 17. *And this I say, that the covenant that was confirmed before of God in Christ, the law which was four hundred and thirty years after, cannot disanull, that it should make the promise of none effect.*

So that this Covenant was long before *Abrahams* Days ; it was made with [*I am,*] who said, *Before Abraham was I am.* Heb. 7. 1, 2.

But this Author is for saving Elect dying Infants by some other Covenant, and not the Covenant of Grace, otherwise he would never have asked such a strange Question as that, *viz.* How were dying Infants saved before *Abraham*'s Days, or before that Covenant was made with him ?

But you shall hear him own, That Infants are saved in the Covenant of Grace made with *Abraham,* with a [not as such] at the end of it ; a Word used by that Party to cover their Insinuations with, until it is worn thread-bare ; it serves instead of a Mental Reservation to them.

2. Saith he, *I never said no Infants were included in the Covenant of Grace God made with* Abraham, *but not as such, no doubt all Elect Persons, both Infants*

Infants and *Adult*, were included in the Covenant of Grace.

Pray obferve here he doth own, that Children are Elected, which is more than fome of his own Perfwafion will grant, that are not Free-willers; and alfo he owns, that Elect Infants are in the Covenant of Grace, and yet not in it, and all in a Breath as it were.

5. In Page aforefaid faith he, *God hath many ways to fave dying Infants, which we know not; he can apply the Benefits and Merits of Chrifts Blood to them in ways we are wholly ignorant of, and ought not to trouble our felves with it: Secret things belong to God; but revealed things to us, and to our children.*

For the confirmation of this, he cites one Dr. *Taylor*.

Pray take notice, how this Man contradicts himfelf; for in Page 21. he faith, *They muft believe and repent, and bring forth good Fruit*; and in Page 25. the Words juft before, he faith, *No doubt all Elect Perfons, both Infants and Adult, are included in the Covenant of Grace:* And yet here he faith, in the fame Page, that God hath many ways to fave dying Infants, which we know not, but are wholly ignorant of it, and ought not to trouble our felves with it: Secret things belong to God; but revealed things belong to us, and our Children.

But before I proceed, I muft take notice of thofe Words of *Mofes*, in *Deut.* 29. 29. with which he covers his many ways of faving dying Infants. *Mofes* in that Chapter had by the Command of God fummoned all the People together, Man, Woman, and Child, to enter into a Covenant with the Lord; and after they had fo done, he tells them in effect, that if they did not keep their Covenant, which was the fame that God

F 4 made

made with *Abraham, Isaac,* and *Jacob,* that then he would bring upon them all the Curses of the Covenant, *Verse* 21. which was a Secret that was wrapt up in the Covenant, which those that were wicked did not mind, and this Secret did belong to God onely to Execute; but the Blessing of the Covenant did belong to those that did make Conscience of keeping the Covenant, and to their Children; not of Merit, but by Grace.

1. Hence we may observe, That Covenant-Mysteries are great Secrets, and belong to none but them which fear the Lord, and their Children, *Psal.* 25. 14. *The secret of the Lord is with them that fear him, and he will shew them his covenant.*

2. None can know those secret Covenant Mysteries, but them which fear the Lord, and their Children.

2. It is a great Mercy to be well acquainted with Covenant Mysteries; and it is a very great Judgment not to be acquainted with them; for it is a sure sign that they do not fear the Lord, because it is said, *The secret of the Lord are with them that fear him,* &c.

4. And Lastly, None can know them but those that God doth discover them unto, by his Word and Spirit.

Surely then it is to be feared, that those Men that Assert, That the Covenant which God made with *Abraham* is dissolved, or that there were two Covenants made with him, and one of them is repealed, are but little acquainted with the Covenant, if not Strangers unto it, otherwise they would not speak so irreverently about it, as they do.

But to proceed, Saith our Author, *There are many ways God hath for the saving of dying Infants, which*

which we are wholly ignorant of, and ought not to trouble our selves with it: *Secret things belong to God*, &c.

1. To this I Answer, That the Salvation of all the Elect of God is Revealed; and Christ faith, *There is nothing covered that shall not be revealed, and hid that shall not be made known.*

2. This is very strange, that there should be so many ways to save dying Infants in, and as strange, that none of them should be made known, and almost as strange, that *A Guide of a Flock* should be ignorant of them all, and declare it in Print to the World, and dehort others from diving into it, as being too secret a thing for them to meddle with; which is very like the *Red-Letter* Guides, which Teach, That Ignorance is the Mother of Devotion: But if Ignorance be the Mother, the Devil is the Father of it.

3. For my part, I never understood there were so many ways to save Elect dying Infants in; therefore before I can set it down, as an Article of my Faith, I must be better satisfied, and not take up in bare Notions, especially when he declares his own Ignorance in this Matter.

4. I cannot find that the Holy Scriptures give any manner of countenance to this new-fashion Doctrine, but on the contrary; for our Saviour Christ tells us but of Two Ways into Eternity, and I am sure he knows best, and but one of them is the Way to Eternal Life, *Matth.* 7. 14. *Because strait is the gate, and narrow is the way which leadeth unto life, and few there be that find it.* There is but one way to Eternal Life and Salvation, (if Christ's own Words may obtain credit,) and that is a *narrow way*; it is not said, Narrow are the ways which lead unto life, which must have been said, had there been more ways than one.

5. Christ

5. Chrift himfelf is this way, as the *broad way* to Hell is through Satan and Unbelief, fo the *narrow way* to Heaven is through Faith in Chrift Jefus, *John* 14. 4, 5, 6. *And whither I go ye know, and the way ye know.*

Thomas faith unto him, Lord, we know not whither thou goeft, and how can we know the way?

Jefus faith unto him, I am the way, and the truth, and the life: no man cometh unto the Father but by me.

6. Therefore if there be more ways to Heaven than one, then there muft be more Chrifts than one; but there is but one Mediator between God and Man, the Man Chrift Jefus; neither is there Salvation in any other; for there is no other name given whereby we may be faved, *Eph.* 4. *One Lord, one faith, one baptifm, One God and Father of all, who is above all, and through all, and in you all.*

There is no faving of any Perfons, Old or Young, without the Grace of Faith, *Mark* 16. 16. *John* 3. 36. Thus you fee there is but one way to Eternal Life, either for Old or Young, and that is through Faith in the Righteoufnefs and Merits of our Lord Jefus Chrift: Therefore Elect dying Infants muft have the Grace of Faith to change their Natures, and be made Partakers of the Divine Nature, otherwife they cannot poffibly be faved, becaufe without Faith it is impoffible to pleafe God.

7. Therefore in the feventh place I challenge him, or any Man elfe of that Opinion, to produce any one way more for the faving Elect dying Infants, than for the faving Adult Believers, inftead of thefe many ways, and I will freely become their Profelyte; for there is no way for the faving any Perfons, but what is revealed in Scripture.   8. This

8. This is very surprizing, that such a Man as this, that is *A Pastor of a Flock*, should be such a Stranger in our *Israel* to these things.

9. These many ways of saving dying Infants, distinct from that of saving Adult Believers, doth contradict Mr. *H. C.* who affirms there was but one way more, and if it had not been one too many, he had been right; for saith he, *We can tell you a better way of washing away of Original sin, namely, by the Imputation of Christ's Righteousness to Infants dying in Infancy*: There wanted but one Ingredient more, namely, the Grace of Faith. I must confess he bid very fair for it, but as good never a whit, as never the better.

10. Do but observe how these two Authors do differ,

(1.) Mr. *H. C.* hath but one way, but Mr. *B. K.* saith, *There are many ways to save dying Infants*.

(2.) Mr. *C.* seems to be very well acquainted with that one way, because he saith, *We can tell ye a better way*, &c. But there was reason enough for it, because it is a way of their own making and devising: But Mr. *K.* is ignorant of all his ways, and the reason may be this, because I find he did not make them himself, but it seems one Dr. *Taylor* made them to his hand, only he makes them his own by quoting and approving of them.

11. These many unknown ways for the saving of Elect Dying Infants is very Apposite and Agreeable to the Two Covenants he affirms God made with *Abraham*, one with his Spiritual Seed, and the other with his Carnal, which is something of kin to Mr. *H. C*'s. Covenant of *peculiarity* made with *Abraham*, and his new-found-way of saving Dying Infants without the Grace of Faith,

Faith, It is all of a piece, and might all do very well, if it were not for one thing, and that is this, *viz.* That it is opposite to the Holy Scriptures.

12. I do readily own that there are two contrary Seeds belonging to *Abraham*, and that these two Seeds of *Abraham* are in two contrary Covenants is unquestionable, and so are the Seed of all Believers, of which *Abrahams* Seed are composed: The Elect Spiritual Seed, those are in the Covenant of Grace, but their Carnal corrupt Seed are all in the Covenant of Works, but that ever God made Two Covenants with *Abraham*, in (*Gen.* 17. 7.) distinct one from another, one for his Spiritual Seed, and the other for his Carnal Seed, I utterly deny.

13. If God made two distinct Covenants with *Abraham* and his Seed, Then,

(1.) There must be that in the one that is peculiar to his Spiritual Seed.

(2.) There must be that in the other that is peculiar to his Carnal Seed; but we find no such Distinction in the Covenant, but it is altogether unscriptural: For,

1. Both the Seeds of *Abraham* had a right to all the External Benefits and Priviledges of the Everlasting Covenant which God made with *Abraham*, very few excepted.

2. As we do not know certainly who are Believers, and who are Unbelievers now under the profession of the Gospel, because sad Experience tells us, That there are many Hypocrites that do partake of all the External Priviledges of the Gospel, and so there were under the *Mosaick* Dispensation; but I can find no Scripture that gives any Manner of Testimony to the making Two Covenants with *Abraham*: Pray look over these Scriptures, and see if you can find any such

thing there, *Gen.* 17. 2, 4, 7, 8, 9, 10, 11, 13, 19, 21. *Deut.* 29. 9, 10, 11, 13, 14. *Pfalm* 105. 8, 9, 10. *Gal.* 3. 16, 17.

14. *Abrahams* Natural Seed were all and to be all in the Covenant of Works, (to be) that is with a refpect to thofe that are not yet born, *viz.* That Covenant which God made with *Adam*; and with Reverence be it fpoken: What need had God to make another Covenant of Works with *Abraham* when that was in Being? And God had no new Terms to add to that Covenant; it is meer non-fence to imagine any fuch thing.

15. That there were two Covenants from *Adam*, to the coming of Chrift, and from thence, to the Converfion of the *Jews*, at Chrift's Second Coming, and to the end of the World I do own, and they are the fame from the making them, as with *Adam*, only that of Works was then broken, though, they have paffed through various Difpenfations and Declarations, but the ftate of both is the fame; *He that believeth fhall be faved, but he that believeth not, fhall be damned*: So it was from *Adam* to this day, and ever will be to the end of the World.

16. All the Race of Mankind (our Saviour Chrift only excepted) were, are, and fhall be conceived in *Adams* firft Covenant, even the very Elect themfelves, but Chrift by his Spirit of Grace takes hold of all the Spiritual Seed of *Abraham* with his merciful hand of Love and Compaffion, and plucks them up by the Roots out of that Covenant, and tranfplants them into the Everlafting Covenant of Grace; for they were given by God the Father from all Eternity unto Chrift as his Seed, *Pfalm* 89. 29. *His Seed alfo will I make to endure for ever, and his Throne as the days of heaven.* *John* 17. 6. *I have manifefted thy Name unto the men which thou gaveft me out of the world:*

Thine they were, and thou gavest them me; and they have kept thy word: They were God the Fathers by Election, and he gave them to Christ to be his, by Redemption.

So that all the Elect of God under the Law were in the Covenant of Grace, which God declared unto *Abraham*, and were all saved in that Covenant, and none else shall be saved, but them which are in that Covenant now under the Gospel, either Old or Young; that is, that are in the Inner Court of that Covenant.

17. I do declare, I am in a straight, between two great Wonders, and I cannot tell which to wonder at most.

1. Whether at the boldness and confidence of these Two Authours in imposing such Fallacious corrupt Doctrines upon the People: Or,

2. At the Peoples Ignorance, to suffer themselves to be so horribly Deluded and Imposed upon; It is a great sign that they are very fond of their own Opinion, that they thus sacrifice their Reason, and also the Truths of God to it.

18. This Authour never repeated the words of the Covenant, though he hath mentioned the Chapter several times, and the Verse once, in which the Covenant is; nay, he hath written the first part of the Verse, until he came to the words, *Everlasting Covenant*, and there he stopt, his Pen would go no farther, as you may see in *page 19*, I will lay down the words at length exactly as they are in his Book.

' *Gen. 17. 7. And I will establish my Covenant*
' *between me and thee, and thy seed after thee in*
' *their generations, &c. And I will give unto thee,*
' *and unto thy seed after thee, the Land wherein*
' *thou art a stranger, all the Land of Canaan, &c.*
' *And ye shall circumcise the flesh of your foreskin,*
' *and*

' *and it shall be a token of the Covenant betwixt me*
' *and you,* verse 11.

Here to make amends for what he left out of the 7*th.* verse, which are the very quintessence of the Covenant; namely, in these words, *For an everlasting Covenant to be a God unto thee and thy seed after thee:* He hath brought on part of the words of the 8*th.* verse, but his Pen would go no farther there neither, but when he come just to *Everlasting possession,* there he makes a halt; But this I note also, the 8*th.* verse is not set down, and then to finish it, he betakes himself to the 11*th.* verse.

So that this looks as if it were a designed contrivance, especially if we consider that he hath not mentioned the *Everlasting Covenant* in all his Book, though he hath quoted, *Gen.* 17. several times, and why he should leave out the main thing in controversie, I will leave the Reader to Judge.

And then to charge People with blindness that could not see two Covenants, is a piece of great presumption; This is the same road by which Popery came into the World, and is now maintained and upheld: O Sirs, have a care that you do not Imbibe such uncouth Notions, and strange Doctrines as these are: But to the Law, and to the Testimony, if they speak not according to this word, it is because there is no Light in them, *Isa.* 8. 20. And see what the Apostle saith in *Gal.* 1. 7. *But though we, or an Angel from heaven, preach any other Gospel unto you, then that which we have preached unto you, let him be accursed.*

19. All these Ceremonies and Sacrifices under the Mosaick Dispensation, were but Types and Shadows of good things to come, but the Gospel was wrapped up in them, and Christ was enjoyed

ed under them; The Law was but the Cabinet, but the Gospel was the Jewel: Therefore these Transient things could be no Essential part of the Covenant, because that is an Everlasting Covenant, ordered in all things, and sure.

20. Though the Form of Circumcision was Transient, and ceased being Abolished with the rest of the Ceremonies, yet the Essential part thereof remaineth in the Flesh; for nothing could be more a Type of Baptisme than Circumcision, because all the Subjects of that Ordinance were passive, as all the Subjects of Baptisme are, and for confirmation of this, do but observe what the Lord hath said in *Gen.* 17. 13. *He that is born in thy house, and he that is bought with thy money, must needs be circumcised, and my Covenant shall be in your flesh for an Everlasting Covenant.*

21. Again the Essential part of Circumcision is to last, as long as the Covenant it self lasteth; because it is the Token, or one of the Seals thereof, which must continue until all Humane Flesh be Dissolved; otherwise how can it be God's Covenant in the Flesh of the Seed of *Abraham*, for an Everlasting Covenant, without any Limitation or Period of time.

22. How could this Token of the Covenant be Everlasting if the Essence thereof was dissolved upon the coming in of the Gospel, this cannot be, for it is a contradiction in it self, for Everlasting and Dissolution, are opposites, therefore I would fain know of our Opponents, what came in the room of Circumcision that supplies the form thereof, if the Ordinance of Baptism doth not; for there must be no Vacancy in the Essential part of the Constitution of a Church, but of necessity there must be something of supplement thereof, and no Ordinance under the Gospel hath

to

e External Fleshy part of Man, but
no Ordinance under the Law
ncision. And for Illustrations sake,
compare it to a standing Office at
s no sooner one Officer is removed
ome other way, but another steps
es his place; therefore some will
Kings never dye: So it was with
for no sooner was that removed by
the Ceremonial Law, but in steps
supplyes its place; for otherwise it
that Circumcision should be for
Covenant in the Flesh of all the
un, both under the Law and Gof-
ffing is come upon the Gentiles.

Seeing that *Abraham shall surely be-
*d mighty nation, and all the nations
ll be blessed in him* ?
ay be Objected, That Baptism can
Antitype of Circumcision, because
lale Children were circumcised?

Answer, The Female were inclu-
h as Man is the Head and Repre-
le Woman, and Woman is a part
taken out from Man, and is bone
ad flesh of his flesh, *Gen.* 2. 23.
27. *And God said, Let us make man
fter our likeness: and let them have
e fish of the sea*, &c.
ere is the Woman wrapped up in
his Phrase, [*Let us make man, and
ominion.*]
*d man in his own image, in the image
he him: male and female created he*

oman is included again, in these
created man, &c. *created he him*, &c.
male

male and female created he them. Here is *him*, male and female: So that this cavilling-Objection is Answered; for you see the Woman was of the Man, and not the Man of the Woman, in the first Formation, *Gen.* 27. 21, 22.

2. The Female Seed of *Abraham* are in the Covenant, as well as the Male, otherwise you must deny them to be any part of his Seed; but that Women were in Covenant, both under the Law and Gospel, is clear; for there were Holy Women under the Law, and we read of *Abraham's* Daughters under the Gospel, 1 *Pet.* 3. 5, 6.

3. And lastly, I will quote my old Authour *H. C.* in page 5. of his former Book, where if we may take the words fairly as they are laid down, do clearly and evidently set forth Circumcision, to be a True Type of Baptisme, and came in the room thereof, and is of the same use to the Church, and makes the same Figure in the Gospel-Church Dispensation, as it did in the Church-Dispensation under the Law: The words are as followeth:

'Know therefore ye Servants of the Lord, as
' Circumcision was the Door into the *Jewish*
' Church, which was National, so Baptisme is the
' Door into the Gospel-Church, which is Con-
' gregational.

In my late Book, called, *An Antidote to prevent the Prevalency of Anabaptisme*, &c. In page 18, I made these Observations upon these words aforesaid as followeth,

' Here is Door for Door, or indeed but one and
' the same Door, onely it is hung upon new, and
' also better hinges; but the Door is the same
' still: Now for my part, I must needs own my
' self to be of the same Opinion with this Au-
' thor in this point, And who could ever imagin
that

'that this Person should deny, that Baptism came
'in the room of Circumcision, seeing he hath bid
'so fairly for it; for he hath tacitly asserted,
'that the Ordinance of Baptisme is of the same
'use, and supplies the very same place, and ma-
'keth the very same Figure in the Church now,
'even as Circumcision did in the Church of God
'under the Ceremonial Law; namely the Door
'of Entrance; But however, though he hath
'thus fairly declared, yet he must not abide by
'it, nor allow that Baptisme came in the room
'of Circumcision, because if he had, he must
'allow of Infants Baptisme, but he hath chosen
'rather to contradict himself by his following
'Discourse, in the aforesaid Book, than to allow
'of that.—

Now pray Reader mind what he saith of me about these Observations, in *page 9*, in his pretended Answer unto my Book aforesaid.

2. 'Another strange Position is, because I say,
'That as Circumcision was the Door into the
'*Jewish* Church, which was National, so Baptism
'is the Door into the Gospel-Church, which is
'Congregational: Now this being true in his
'own Opinion, why should it be a strange po-
'sition.

To this I Answer,

1. Negatively, I will not say there is Jesuits Powder in this cunning Reflection:

2. But I will say positively, that there is some of their policy in it; Pray observe, he doth not say positively, neither at the beginning, nor in the Conclusion, where he mentions the word strange position, that I did say so, but he hath done it by a sly Fallacious Insinuation; for I challenge him to prove that ever I called that a *strange position* in all my Book aforesaid; and if
he

he can, I will acknowledge it to be a fault publickly; for it is the only Pofition I liked in both his Books: For it is my own Judgment and Opinion, That it is fo; and for that Reafon it was very unlikely that I fhould count it to be a ftrange Pofition, therefore I am calumniated by him.

24. Now in the laft place I have with all perfpicuity and plainnefs given you my Thoughts concerning the Covenant which God made with *Abraham, Ifaac,* and *Jacob,* and their Seed after them in their Generations, which Covenant devolved upon us *Gentiles,* and all our Children, *Acts* 3. 25. *Ye are the children of the Prophets, and of the Covenant which God made with our Fathers, faying unto Abraham, And in thy feed fhall all the kindreds of the Earth be bleffed:* And this Bleffing came upon the *Gentiles* in the Apoftles time; and though the Difpenfation was changed, yet the Covenant it felf was never altered, nor taken up by the Root; for all Believing *Gentiles*, and all their Seed are as much included in it as ever the *Jews* and their Children were, as I have clearly proved: For Chrift was and is the Head, and Reprefentative of all the Elect Covenant Seed, both under the Law, and under the Gofpel; for all were, and all are, and all fhall be, Members of Chrifts Myftical Body, *The Church:* Therefore not one Grain of that Seed fhall ever fall to the Ground and be loft: Thus you fee the Covenant which God made with *Abraham* and all his Seed, both Spiritual and Carnal, ftands Faft and Firm to Gofpel-Believers, and all their Seed, both Spiritual and Carnal; notwithftanding *Hercules* hath been *Mawling* of it with his *Club*, and *Benjamin* hewing at it with his *Broad Axe*, they cannot deftroy it, becaufe it is an *Everlafting Covenant*;

neither

neither can they come at it, so much as to touch it, For Christ saith, The Gates of Hell shall not prevail against his Church; and (that) stands in the Covenant, and the Covenant in that; neither can they cut off any of the Branches of it; for that is Christ's Prerogative, if they prove to be Dead Branches, as all the Carnal Seed are, *John* 15. 1, 2.

This Broad-side hath sunk and destroyed all their Invincible *Armado*, consisting of Florid Syllogistical Arguments, Specious Allegations, fallacious Notions, and crafty Positions, and corrupt, gilded, false Doctrines, together with all their foul Practices; and they are fallen into the Pit they digged for us and our Children, themselves; for instead of unchurching the Infant Seed of Believers, by which they must have unchurched their Parents also, they have very fairly and clearly unchurched themselves, and that by their own Arguments made use of to maintain their Opinion by; therefore the one may hang up his *Club*, and the other may lay aside his *Axe*, and both betake themselves to some other kind of Tools and Instruments, that they know better how to make use of; for these you see will not do.

Now upon the whole Matter, let any spiritually wise Man judge, whether this Opinion of theirs be such an indifferent harmless Opinion, that must have so many Fulsome Errours to support it, for I can appeal to God, Angels, and Men, Aye, and to their own Books too, that I have not wronged them in the least in any point, unless it hath been in this, *viz.* to confute their Intollerable Errours by Scripture Truths; but if that be to wrong them, I will wrong them again, unless they come off from their Erroneous Principles,

and

and no longer thus deceive and delude the People, by leading them in Ignorance concerning Covenant Myſteries, *Pſal.* 25. 14. And this I can alſo truly ſay, that what I have written, I have not done it out of any baſe ſiniſter End, or for Applauſe, but in ſincerity and uprightneſs of Heart, primarily and purely to vindicate the Honour and Glory of God's Free Grace, which this Opinion of theirs doth Impede and Eclipſe, and ſubordinately for the good of poor miſguided Souls.

But however if they do think, I have done either their Perſons, or their Opinion any wrong, the *Preß* ſtands open, and I am ready to ſatisfie them, and ſo let them vindicate themſelves if they can, and clear themſelves of what I have charged them with; but if not, my Advice unto them is, that they would come off from that Opinion. It will be no diſhonour unto them; for it is but to Face to the Right as you were, many of you that are Leaders: And although I dare not ſay but there are many Gracious Souls amongſt you, yet this I will ſay, they are better than their Opinion, and they will be ſaved, *yet ſo, as by fire*, 1 Cor. 3. 12, 15.

III.

And *Laſtly*, I am now come to Treat with my Beloved *Conferencers*, which Conference we had together in *London*, on *June* 2. 1693. to whom I muſt give all due perſonal Reſpects, if it were but for their venerable Carriage and Deportment towards me in the management of the aforeſaid Conference, and againſt whom it cannot be imagined that I could have the leaſt perſonal prejudice, by thoſe my ſaid Friends themſelves therein in concerned, especially one of them who is my Intimate Bosome Friend, and therefore I will deal faithfully and plainly with them, and I shall not spare them, and that because I love them; for he that is a Man's true Friend will not suffer him to go on hood-winkt towards a Precipice, and not stop him if he can, to prevent his distruction; a skilful Chyrurgion will cut off a Gangreen'd Limb to save the Patient's Life; an Errour in Judgment is a Spiritual Gangreen in a Man's Soul, and if it be not cured, it may destroy him, Body and Soul: Therefore, under these Considerations aforesaid, they cannot take it amiss if I touch them to the Quick; for my part, I was never good at flattering nor dissembling in my Life, and I am now grown too old to learn.

Secondly, Here will also fall in an Answer to a Letter I received, since I have been writing this Book, from one Mr. *James Jordan* of *Rochester*, an *Anabaptist*: But what Figure he maketh among that People I know not, but I perceive by his writing, that he is an honest well-meaning Man; but he is one that hath more Zeal for his Opinion than Knowledge of the Deep Mysteries of the Covenant of Grace, as will appear when I come to the Touch-stone with him to try his Matter.

But to proceed, I shall begin with my *London* Friends, and lay down the Heads of their Positions, and Reflect upon them in Order, as followeth:

1. They Asserted, That the Covenant God made with *Abraham*, and his Seed, in *Gen.* 17. 7. was but a temporal conditional Covenant.

2. That all Young Infants, of all Nations and People, dying in their Infancy, are saved.

3. That

3. That all dying Infants are saved, but none of them Elected.

4. That all dying Infants are saved, but not Regenerated and born again.

5. That all dying Infants are saved without the Grace of Faith.

6. That all dying Infants are saved, but not sanctified.

7. That all dying Infants are saved without being in a State of Grace.

8. That all dying Infants are saved without being in the Covenant of Grace.

9. And Lastly, Notwithstanding all these corrupt *Arminian* Tenets and Doctrines, they pretended to hold, that the Grace of God is Free, which contradicted all they said.

1. They Asserted, That the Covenant which God made with *Abraham*, and his Seed, in *Gen.* 17. 7. was but a temporal conditional Covenant: The plain English of which is, that it was but a Covenant of Works; neither better nor worse.

2. And that it consisted onely of External Blessings and Priviledges, namely, Ceremonies, Sacrifices, and the Land of *Canaan*, &c.

3. And Lastly, That this Covenant continued no longer then the Ceremonial Law continued, and then it was abolished, and the new Covenant in *Heb.* 8. took place; this, said they, was the Extent of that Covenant which God made with *Abraham*, and all his Seed, neither was there any Benefit or Blessing Entailed upon Gospel believing Gentiles, nor their Posterity, in all that Covenant.

To which I Answer,

First, I do readily grant, that Circumcision, the Passover, and the Land of *Canaan*, &c. were

contained

contained in the Everlasting Covenant which God made with *Abraham*, and there were Conditions also, but I have already said, that there is an Inside and an Out-side to the Covenant, an Inner-court and an Outward-court ; for all are not *Israel* that are of *Israel*, neither is that Circumcision that is not of the Heart, whose Praise is not of God, but of Men : And as for the Conditions of the Covenant, Christ performed that upon the Cross for all those in the In-side, or Inner-court of the Covenant, *Col.* 1. 20, 21. But they which are on the Out-side, or in the Outer-court thereof,, Christ leaves them to perform the Conditions thereof themselves. But I have sufficiently answered and confuted all these Solutions of theirs, already, concerning the Covenant which God made with *Abraham*, therefore I shall proceed to treat about that which is called the *new covenant* in *Heb.* 8. which they affirmed took place at the Abolition of the old one, when the Gospel came in.

1. In the first place I do readily grant, that the Covenant did come under a new Dispensation,, and that the old way of Dispensation was abolished at the coming in of the Gospel; but that the Covenant and the Promise thereof stood fixed and firm, I have clearly proved : Pray look into *Rom.* 11. and *Acts* 2. 38, 39. and *Eph.* 3. 6. *Acts* 10. 45. *Col.* 1. 25, 26, 27. And how could the Blessing of *Abraham* come upon the Gentiles if *Abraham*'s Covenant was abolished ? *Gal.* 3. 28, 29. *Gal.* 4. 28.

2. Let us lay down the Words of the Covenant, which are as followeth, *Heb.* 8. *For finding fault with them, he saith, Behold, the days come (saith the Lord) when I will make a new covenant with the house of Israel and with the house of Judah.*

For this is the covenant that I will make with the house of Israel after those days, faith the Lord; I will put my laws into their mind, and write them in their hearts: and I will be to them a God, and they shall be to me a people.

For I will be merciful to their unrighteousness, and their sins and their iniquities I will remember no more.

Now for Explication.

1. I do believe that this *new covenant*, or rather, a new Dispensation thereof, might have a respect to two sorts of Persons, namely, Jews and Gentiles, and at two certain Periods: (1.) It might have a respect to the Gentiles, at their Call and Conversion to Christ, at the coming in of the Gospel, into which Covenant they were then taken, *Rom.* 11. 17. the Blessing of *Abraham* being then come upon the Gentiles; for the Gentiles were taken into the very same Covenant, and do partake of the same Priviledges with the Jews that stood, and their Seed, which was *Abraham's* Covenant.

And if some of the branches be broken off, and thou being a wild olive-tree wert graffed in amongst them, and with them partakest of the root and fatness of the olive-tree.

Now this must needs be a new Covenant to the Gentiles, because they were never in it before.

2. But Secondly, and more especially, I do believe it concerns the *Hebrews*, whose Fore-fathers had sinned themselves out of the Covenant, which were the Natural Branches of that Blessed Olive-tree, *Rom.* 11. 20, 21, 22. And they are to be taken into this new Dispensation of the Covenant again, at the end of the Days of their Captivity, when the Lord shall open their Eyes, and soften their Hearts, and cleanse them from all their filthyness, *Rom.* 11. 24, 25, 26.

3. This

3. This Covenant will be new to them in several respects: (1.) It will be a new Covenant unto them, because they never were in it before: (2.) It will be a new Covenant to the Jews with a respect to the Frame of it; for it will be such a Frame, as they shall never sin, so as to provoke God to cast them out of it again, as he did their Fore-fathers: (3.) It will be new in this respect also, That the People shall be more holy under that Dispensation of the Covenant then ever their Fore-fathers were, *Zech.* 14. 20, 21.

4. It will be a new Covenant in this respect, that the Special Presence of the Mediatour of the Covenant, our Lord Jesus Christ, will be so enjoyed, in such a Glorious manner, as he never was enjoyed before.

5. And Lastly, This Dispensation of the Covenant will be new to the Jews with a respect unto that Exuberant Light, that shall then flow forth, and accompany it, *Isa.* 60. 1, 3. *Arise, shine, for thy light is come, and the glory of the Lord is risen upon thee.*

And the Gentiles shall come to thy light, and Kings to the brightness of thy rising.

Isa. 30. *Moreover the light of the moon shall be as the light of the sun, and the light of the sun shall be seven fold, as the light of seven days, in the day that the Lord bindeth up the breach of his people, and healeth the stroke of their wound.*

This great conflux of Light is to commence and take place when God converts the Jews to the Christian Faith, and restores their own Land to them, and forms them into Government, both of Church and State, which these two great Lights are to Accommodate, that of the Sun the Church, and that of the Moon their Civil State: So that this is the same Covenant State that God

made

made with *Abraham* and his Seed, that is here called a new Covenant in *Heb.* 8. which is taken almoſt *verbatim* out of *Jer.* 31. 31. *Behold, the days come, ſaith the Lord, that I will make a new covenant with the houſe of Iſrael, and with the houſe of Judah:*

Verſe 32. *Not according to the covenant that I made with their fathers in the day that I took them by the hand, to bring them out the land of Egypt (which my covenant they brake, although I was an husband unto them, ſaith the Lord:)*

From hence we may obſerve Three Things; the 1. is this, That they broke Covenant with God; for God never breaks Covenant with any: 2. They were in a very near Relation to God; for they were married unto him; for he was an Husband unto them: 3. And Laſtly, For their Idolatry, which is Spiritual Adultery, God gave them a Bill of Divorcement.

Verſe 33. *But this ſhall be the covenant that I will make with the houſe of Iſrael, After thoſe days, ſaith the Lord,* (this muſt be after the Days of their Captivity,) *I will put my law in their inward parts, and write it in their hearts, and will be their God, and they ſhall be my people.*

Verſe 34. *And they ſhall teach no more every man his neighbour, and every man his brother, ſaying, Know the Lord: for they ſhall all know me, from the leaſt of them unto the greateſt of them, ſaith the Lord: for I will forgive their iniquity, and I will remember their ſin no more.*

2. Here you may obſerve from theſe Two Propheſies, *Jer.* 31. and *Heb.* 8. 11, 12. that the Teaching and Knowledge of God, is the Fruit and Effects of pardoning Love and Grace, and of God's being merciful to the unrighteouſneſs both of Old and Young, Original Sins and Actual

Tranſgreſſions, Original Sins to Young Babes, and Original and Actual Sins and Tranſgreſſions to Adult Elect Sinners; for God faith, that *all ſhall know me, from the leaſt of them to the greateſt of them:* God begins firſt with the leaſt. Here is a ſufficient Proof, had we no other, that the Children of believing Parents are in the Covenant with their Parents under this new Diſpenſation thereof.

3. All you that Aſſert, Children are not capable of knowing the Lord, nor of being taught by him, nor that they are in Covenant, nor of receiving the Grace of Faith, by which God is to be ſeen, who is Inviſible to an Eye of Sence.

O! that you would often think upon theſe Conditions of the new Diſpenſations of the Covenant, which Conditions a Young Child is as capable of performing, as any Adult Perſon is whatſoever: For it is the Lord's [*I will,*] and [*they ſhall;*] *for they ſhall all know me,* faith the Lord, *from the leaſt of them to the greateſt of them;* that is, from the youngeſt, or leaſt Child amongſt them, to the oldeſt Man or Woman: *For this is life eternal to know thee the true God, and Jeſus Chriſt whom thou haſt ſanctified and ſent.*

4. My Beloved, Now I hope you ſee God hath prevented you of cutting off the Intail of the Infant Seed of Believers, and from depriving them of their Covenant Intereſt.

5. Suppoſe (for Arguments ſake) that, for once, I ſhould grant you, that the Covenant which God made with *Abraham* and his Seed, had been ſuch a Covenant as you would fain have it to be, and that it was aboliſhed at the coming in of the Goſpel, as you Aſſert it was, and that this new Covenant in *Jer.* 31. and *Heb.* 8. came in the room thereof, and did then take place, yet you ſee

see this would not do; for this new Covenant is every whit as merciful to Little Children of believing Parents, as ever that you count the Old one was; for Young Infants are in it, as well as Adult Persons, both of Jews and Gentiles: Here is New *Jerusalem* come down from Heaven, who is the Mother of us all, with all her Children round about her, in this Covenant, and not one lacking, Old or Young.

So that take it in which sense you please, and neither of them will Answer your End; but they are both against you, supposing them to be two, but the Covenant is one and the same, though under another Dispensation; for all the Children of godly Parents are included in both these Dispensations of the Covenant, as I have proved it to be, and not two distinct Covenants, as you vainly conceit them to be. Where are ye now Sirs! and what Refuge will you fly to next? For this is destroyed, and I am resolved to follow you: for you see you are beset; take which Covenant you please, according to your own Notion, and you will find Children in them both.

6. It is very observable in this, that God hath that Tender Care, Honour, and Respect, for the Young Babes of his People, as that they are placed first in Order in the Prophecy, both by the Prophet, and the Apostle, in these Words, *For [all] shall know me, from the least of them to the greatest of them, saith the Lord.* Here we can say, [thus faith the Lord,] and then no matter what Men say to contradict it: There can be none less than Young Children; for they must be the least of them; and, unless you can find any less than the least, your Cause is lost and defunct.

7. That this Prophecy doth principally concern the Jews, is most evident from *Jer.* 31. and
Heb.

Heb. 8. though not wholly to exclude the Gentiles.

Behold, the days come, faith the Lord, that I will make a new covenant with the house of Israel, and with the house of Judah: (Here is not one Word of the Gentiles.) *Not according to the covenant that I made with their fathers in the day that I took them by the hand, to bring them out of the land of Egypt.* Compare *Heb.* 8. 9.

Now that this was spoken to, and of the Jews, will evidently appear, if we confider three things, 1. That the Gentiles were no part of the House of *Israel* and *Judah*: 2. That the Gentiles were none of the Jews Fathers: 3. God did not take the Gentiles by the Hand, and bring them out of *Egypt*; but God destroyed the Gentiles for pursuing the Jews, to bring them back into Captivity again, when God was leading them out of it; for the *Egyptians* were Gentiles; for all that were not Jews, were Gentiles.

2. That this Dispensation could not have its Intire Accomplishment at the coming in of the Gospel, is most certain; for there was not that universal Knowledge of God then amongst the Jews, as there will be under this Dispensation; for there were many Thousands of them in that Day broke off, and cast out of Covenant, for their Unbelief and Ignorance of God; but God hath, and ever will have, a Covenant People in all Ages, to hold up his Name and Honour in the World; because he is ever mindful of his Covenant.

8. And Lastly, That this New Covenant Dispensation will take place at the Second Coming of Christ, at which coming he will destroy Antichrist, 2 *Thess.* 2. 8, 9. and convert the Jews, *Ezek.* 37. 12, 13, 14, 15.

Let us for the Proof of this consider several Texts of Scripture.

1. In *Jer.* 31. out of which the New Covenant is quoted, *Verses* 1, 8, 9, 10, 11. *At the same time, saith the Lord, will I be the God of all the families of Israel, and they shall be my people.*

Behold, I will bring them from the north-countrey, and gather them from the coasts of the earth, and with them the blind and the lame, the woman with child, and her that travaileth with child together, a great company shall return thither.

They shall come with weeping, and with supplications will I lead them: I will cause them to walk by the rivers of waters, in a straight way wherein they shall not stumble: for I am a father to Israel, and Ephraim is my first-born.

Hear the word of the Lord, O ye nations, and declare it in the isles afar off, and say, He that scattered Israel will gather him, and keep him, as a shepherd doth his flock.

For the Lord hath redeemed Jacob, and ransomed him from the hand of him that was stronger than he.

We the Inhabitants of these Isles are commanded to declare this Great Truth, namely, of the Jews Conversion; and I do believe it is better known, and more declared, in these Isles, and their Appendix, than in all the World besides, *Psal.* 65. 5, 8.

2. A Second Scripture is in *Isa.* 43. 5, 6. *Fear not, for I am with thee: I will bring thy seed from the east, and gather thee from the west.*

I will say to the north, Give up; and to the south, Keep not back: bring my sons from far, and my daughters from the ends of the earth.

3. A Third Scripture is in *Ezek.* 24. *Therefore will I save my flock, and they shall no more be a prey; and I will judge between cattel and cattel.*

And

And I will set up one shepherd over them, and he shall feed them, even my servant David, he shall feed them, and he shall be their shepherd:

And the Lord will be their God, and my servant David a prince among them; I the Lord have spoken it. This cannot be meant of David literally and properly; but mystically it is Christ.

And I will make with them a covenant of peace, and I will cause the evil beasts to cease out of the land, and they shall dwell safely, &c.

Thus shall they know, that I the Lord their God am with them, and that they, even the house of Israel, are my people, saith the Lord.

4. A Fourth Scripture is in *Jer.* 23. 3, 5, 6. *And I will gather the remnant of my flock, out of all countries whither I have driven them, and I will bring them again to their folds, and they shall be fruitful and increase.*

Behold, the days come, saith the Lord, that I will raise unto David a righteous branch, and a king shall reign and prosper, and shall execute judgment and justice in the earth.

In his days Judah shall be saved, and Israel shall dwell safely: and this is his name whereby he shall be called, THE LORD OUR RIGHTEOUSNESS. This is a Title peculiar to our Lord Jesus Christ.

5. And Lastly, To name no more, *Ezek.* 36. *For I will take you from among the heathen, and gather you out of all countries, and will bring you into your own land.*

Then will I sprinkle clean water upon you, and ye shall be clean: from all your filthiness, and from all your idols will I cleanse you.

A new heart also will I give you, and a new spirit will I put within you, and I will take away the stony heart out of your flesh, and I will give you an heart of flesh.

And I will put my Spirit within you, and cause you to walk in my Statutes, and ye shall keep my Judgments, and do them.

And ye shall dwell in the Land that I gave to your Fathers, and ye shall be my People, and I will be your God.

Thus you see clearly that the New Dispensation of the Covenant will take place in special manner at the Coming of Christ, and the Conversion of the Jews; which I do both hope and believe is very near; and it is my Opinion, that God hath taken Peace from the Earth, *Rev.* 6: 4. and will never restore it again until the Restitution of all Things, *Acts* 3. 20, 21. And then it will be a most Glorious Time, such as never yet was in the World since the Creation thereof. It is a very great Error for People to Assert, That the World will be at an end when the Jews are converted: Pray read *Zech.* 8. 3, 4, 5, 6, 7, 8.

2. I will give you my Reason, why I do hope, and believe, that the Coming of Christ, and the Destruction of Antichrist is near, even at the Door; because we have been, and still are under such eminent conspicuous Fulfilling the Signs of those Times, under which Christ himself hath commanded us, saying, *And when these things begin to come to pass, then look up, and lift up your heads; for your redemption draweth nigh,* Luke 21. 28. And we are commanded also to watch for the coming of our Lord, *Rev.* 16. 15.

3. And Lastly, I will take notice of some of the Signs, that are as so many Prodromes to give us notice of the near Approach of our Lord.

1. There is greater Light and Knowledge of these Mysteries before they come to pass, *Dan.* 12. 1, 2, 3, 4.

2. There is an earnest Expectation of its coming to

to pass a little before it doth come to pass by some, not many; the number of these will be but very small, compared to the rest of the Christians, in which there is also a Sign, *Luke* 18. 2, 3, 4, 5, 6, 7, 8.

4. Another Sign is in *Mal.* 3. 15. *And now we call the proud happy: yea, they that work wickedness are set up; yea, they that tempt God are even delivered.*

5. Here are Three Signs in one, *viz.* Treachery, Bribery and Hypocrisie, *Job* 15. 34. *For the congregation of hypocrites shall be desolate, and fire shall consume the tabernacles of bribery.* Verse 35. *They conceive mischief, and bring forth vanity, and their belly prepareth deceit.* Psal. 26. 5, 10.

6. Another Sign of Christ's near Approach is the Great Wars, both by Sea and Land, and the Distress of Nations, *Luke* 21. *And there shall be signs in the sun, and in the moon, and in the stars; and upon the earth distress of nations, with perplexity, the sea and the waves roaring; Mens hearts failing them for fear, and for looking after those things which are coming on the earth; for the powers of heaven shall be shaken.* That is Church Powers: But it shall be but shaken; it shall not be broken, nor taken up by the Root, but is in imminent danger, and must be cleansed and refined as with a Refiners Fire and Fullers Sope. *And then shall they see the son of man coming in a cloud with power and great glory,* Acts 2. 19, 20, 21. Nahum. 1. 2, 3, 4, 5, 6, 8, 9, 13.

7. Another Infallible Sign is Frequent Earthquakes in divers Places, and in terrible manner, of which we have heard of many these two last Years past. God preserve *England* from the like of that at *Sicilia*.

8. An

8. An Eighth Sign is Pestilence, Raged very much in the *West-Indies.*

9. The strange Vicissitudes, and [turning Providential Dispensations t will be in the World, *Psal.* 75. B judge: *he putteth down one, and settet For in the hand of the Lord there is a wine is red: it is full of mixture, and of the same: but the dregs thereof a of the earth shall wring them out, and All the horns of the wicked also will the horns of the righteous shall be exa* 1. 18, 19, 20, 21.

10. Another Sign of Christ's comi Antichrist is in *Hag.* 2. *For thus saith hosts, Yet once, it is a little while, and the heavens, and the earth, and the dry land: And I will shake all nations, sire of all nations shall come, and I wil with glory, saith the Lord of hosts..* Church, which is the House of God.

11. Another Sign of the coming of great decay of Trade, and great Tr by Sea and Land, *Zech.* 8. 10. *Fo days,* (that is, the Days of Christ's S ing and Appearance,) *there was no nor any hire for beast,* (which signifi decay of Trade,) *neither was there any that went out, or came in, because of* t This may signifie the great Hazard an Sea, both with a respect to Merchant ners, and the greatest danger is just ing out and returning home in the Cl Channel.

12. Another Sign is the cruel D and Conflagrations by Fire and Swo *For behold, the Lord will come with fu*

his chariots like a whirlwind, to render his anger with fury, and his rebuke with flames of fire. For by fire, and by sword, will the Lord plead with all flesh: and the slain of the Lord shall be many. And look into the 8, 9, 10, 11, 12. *verses* of the same *Chapter*, and there you may see the Conversion of the Jews, and the Fulness of the Gentiles predicted.

Now let us consider whether ever there was so much Fire used in Wars, both by Sea and Land, as there is now, witness the Bombarding so many Places upon the Land, and the Burning so many Ships at Sea ; wherefore I think this may pass for as clear a Sign as any of the rest.

13. There is another Sign in being, which is of the near Approach of the Destruction of Antichrist, and that is the Three Fold Division, and what that Division is I must leave to the consideration of the Reader ; I shall onely lay down the Prophecy, which is in *Rev.* 16. 19. *And the great city was divided into three parts, and the cities of the nations fell: and great Babylon came in remembrance before God, to give unto her the cup of the wine of the fierceness of his wrath.*

14. Another Sign of the Coming of Christ is mocking and scoffing at Piety and Holiness, and even at the Coming of Christ also, which is a Sin very common among Protestants, as well as others : 2 *Pet.* 3. 3. *Knowing this first, that there shall come in the last days scoffers,* (that is, in the last days of Antichrist's Reign, and first before Christ comes,) *walking after their own lusts, and saying, Where is the promise of his coming ? for since the fathers fell asleep, all things continue as they were from the beginning of the creation. For this they willingly are ignorant of,* &c.

15. Ano-

15. Another Sign is great Divisions, the Father against the Son, and the Son against the Father, the Mother-in-law against the Daughter-in-law, and the Daughter-in-law against her Mother-in-law, and Brother against Brother, &c. Witness *Whiggs* and *Tories*.

16. Another Sign is when People grow Incorrigible under the Judgments of God, *Isa.* 26. 11, 21. *Lord, when thy hand is lifted up, they will not see: but they shall see, and be ashamed for their envy at the people, yea the fire of thine enemies shall devour them.*

For behold, the Lord cometh out of his place to punish the inhabitants of the earth for their iniquity: the earth also shall disclose her blood, and shall no more cover her slain.

17. Another is Famine, *Mark* 13. 8.

18. Another sure Sign of the near Approach of Christ is the great Inundation of all manner of Wickedness and Ungodliness, *Joel* 3. *Put ye in the sickle, for the harvest is ripe; come, get ye down, for the preß is full, the fats overflow, for their wickedneß is great.* I believe the Fats do overflow now, or at least begin so to do. *The Lord also shall rore out of Zion, and utter his voice from Jerusalem, and the heavens and the earth shall shake; but the Lord will be the hope of his people, and the strength of the children of Israel, So shall ye know that I am the Lord your God dwelling in Zion, my holy mountain: then shall Jerusalem be holy; and there shall no strangers paß through her any more.* This is a clear Prediction of the Conversion of the Jews, when God will thus destroy the wicked.

19. Another Sign is the carnal, drowsie, sleepy Frame of Heart, that the wise Virgins are sunk down into, as well as the foolish, *Mat.* 25. 5. *While the bridegroom tarried, they all slumbred and slept.*

slept. Mat. 24. *But as the days of Noe were, so shall also the coming of the Son of man be. For as in the days that were before the flood, they were eating and drinking, marrying and giving in marriage, until the day that Noe entred into the ark, And knew not until the flood came, and took them all away; so shall also the coming of the Son of man be.* Chrift will come in a furprizing way, even as a Thief in the Night; and therefore our great Duty is to watch for the coming of our Lord, that his Coming may not be furprizing to us; but be our rejoicing, Rev. 16. 15. *Behold, I come as a thief. Blessed is he that watcheth, and keepeth his garments, lest he walk naked, and they see his shame.*

20. And Laftly, Which is the laft Sign that I shall name, and it will be the laft Sign alfo that will be fulfilled, and that is in Zech. 14. 6, 7. *And it shall come to pass in that day, that the light shall not be clear, nor dark. But it shall be one day which shall be known to the Lord, not day, nor night: but it shall come to pass that at evening-time it shall be light.*

This ftrange Day which fhall be known to the Lord, feems as if it was known to the Lord only, and that People fhould not know it certainly when they are in it; and that this day is to laft until Chrift cometh, is clear from the foregoing verfe; wherein I humbly conceive is contained a Threatning againft the Wicked in thefe words, *And ye shall flee to the valley of the Mountains, for the valley of the mountains shall reach unto Azal: Yea, Ye shall flee like as ye fled from before the Earth-quake in the days of Uzziah, King of Judah, And the Lord my God shall come, and all the Saints with thee,* Amos 1. 1, 2. Joel. 3. 16, 17.

This ftrange Day, which is neither Day nor Night

Night confifts of a complication of various Providential Difpenfations, both of Mercy and Judgments, and of the ftrange Principles, Practices, Manners, and Behaviour of Men both Good and Bad, efpecially Men of Figure, and of Men in Confederacyes of contrary Principles one to the other, as *Turks*, *Papifts*, and *Proteftants*; juft like the Feet, and Toes of *Nebuchadnezzars* Image, if not the fame, Dan. 2. 42, 43. *And as the Toes of the Feet were part of Iron, and part of clay, fo the Kingdom, fhall be partly ftrong and partly broken*; This Kingdom is the Kingdom of Antichrift, of which *France* is a part, and the ftrongeft part of it too, and this is to be juft before its utter down-fall, *And whereas thou faweft Iron mixt with miry Clay, they fhall mingle themfelves with the Seed of men, but they fhall not cleave one to another, even as iron is not mixed with clay*. Dan. 8. *He fhall alfo ftand up againft the Prince of Princes, but he fhall be broken without hands*: I think it is evident enough that the *French* King is guilty of this moft horrible fin, and he may fhare with his Father Antichrift in this Threatning.

Now I pray you confider of all thefe figns, and look abroad, and at home, and fee if you can find any of thefe figns, if not moft or all of them; and if you can then mind what our Saviour Chrift faith in *Mark* 13. 29. *So ye in like manner, when ye fhall fee thefe things come to pafs, know that it is nigh, even at the doors.*

Thus I have given you my Thoughts about the New Difpenfation of the Covenant, when it will principally come to pafs, and who are chiefly concerned therein, namely the *Jews*, though the *Gentiles* alfo, yet more remotely.

2. To

2. To proceed to their Second Position which was this, *That all dying Infants are saved, without any Exception or Restriction;* so that the Children of *Turks*, *Negroes*, *Pagans*, and all other *Infidels* whatsoever, born in Wedlock, or out of Wedlock, have all as great a Priviledge, as the Children of Christian Parents, and they ground this Position upon the Words of the Apostle in 1 *Cor.* 15. 21, 22. *For since by man came Death, by Man came also the Resurrection of the Dead. For as in Adam all die, so even in Christ shall all be made alive*: Thus the Apostle Argued to prove the Resurrection; for it seems there were some among them, that denyed the Resurrection of the Dead; so that this [all that are to be made alive by Christ] are all Good and Bad, Saints and Sinners at the General Day of the Resurrection; so that those all that are to be made alive, shall not all be saved; for then Redemption would be as large as Creation; so that this Scripture doth not Relieve them at all.

2. If all Dying Infants are in the Line of Election, then they shall come within the verge of Salvation; And if so, then are they all given by God the Father unto Christ to Redeem and Save, *John* 17. 9, 10, 11. And Christ is formed in them, but otherwise, this position of our Opponents is a meer Fictitious Empty Notion. But of this more under the next head.

3. In the third place, for a farther prosecution of this Groundless Opinion, Let us bring it to the Touchstone of Gods Word, and try, Whether ever there was any such Universal Provision made for the Salvation of all Dying Infants, *viz. Turks*, *Negroes*, *Pagans*, and all other Infidels whatsoever.

And for the Tryal of this, I wi
Three remarkable Difpenfations o
and Fury: And let us obferve from
may be inferr'd for the confuting
Error.
1. The Firſt is in that Commiſ
unto the Prophet *Ezekiel.* 2. in t
of the City of *Sodom.* 3. And la
Gods drowning the whole World,
Family only excepted.

1. I will begin firſt with that I
God's Wrath, in *Ezek.* 9. 6. *Slay*
young, both Maids and Little Childre
but come not near any Man upon whoi
and begin at my Sanctuary.

Thus you fee what the Extent
miſſion was: From whence we may
things:

1. That all were to be deſtroye
man and Child, that were not ma
ſervation.

2. That all Gods Elect were m
ſervation at that time of the Execu
Wrath and Fury; or whenever it r
ted again, which feems as if it w
Iſa. 26. 20, 21. *Rev.* 7. 2, 3.

But there was a fpecial Charge g
ecutioners of God's Wrath and Fur
as to come near thoſe on whom the

3. And laſtly, They were to b
Hypocrites and Formaliſts, which
of that Phraſe, *viz.* Begin at my S
ſo will the Wrath of God Impendir
Houſe of God, but not in the Houſe
17. *For the time is come that judgme*
the houſe of God; and if it firſt begin
the end be of them that obey not the

2 *Theff.* 1. 7, 8. *And to you who are troubled, reſt with us, when the Lord Jeſus ſhall be revealed from Heaven with his mighty Angels, in flaming fire, taking vengeance on them that know not God, and that obey not the Goſpel of our Lord Jeſus Chriſt: The Wine-preſs of God's Wrath is to be trodden without the City,* Rev. 14. 19, 20.

2. The Second Diſpenſation of Gods Wrath was that in the Deſtruction of the City of *Sodom* by fire from Heaven; no doubt, but there were ſome Thouſands of Little Children in all that City, although the *Anabaptiſts* will not allow that there were any Children among thoſe many; nay perhaps Thouſands of whole Houſholds that were Baptized in the Apoſtles time.

1. In the firſt place, Let us obſerve what paſt between God and *Abraham* about deſtroying or ſparing of *Sodom*, before it was deſtroyed.
 1. Therefore I will lay down the Scripture wherein is contained the Threatning of God againſt *Sodom*.
 2. *Abrahams* Interceſſion.
 3. God's Condeſcenſion.
 4. And laſtly, God's Execution.
  1. Here was the Threatning, in *Gen.* 18. 20, 21.
  2. Here was *Abraham's* Interceſſion, in Verſes 26, 28, 29, 30, 31, 32. Pray obſerve how great the Condeſcenſion of God was, for if there could have been found but Ten Righteous Perſons in the whole City, God would have ſpared it.
  2. We may obſerve four things.
   1. Faithful *Abraham* was not for ſlaying the Righteous with the Wicked, as may be ſeen in his Petition to God.
   2. You have God anſwering his Petition.
   3. If all theſe young Infants were ſaved that were ſlain, then their Original Sins were pardoned and
   ſub-

subdued and their Natures changed and made Partakers of the Divine Nature; and then Christ was formed in them, and they were justified by his Righteousness imputed unto them through Faith; and if so, who could be more Righteous than such Children?

4. And lastly, This must be the Natural Consequence; either there were not Ten Children in all the City, or this New-found Doctrine is False, or the Word of God is not true; but it is Blasphemy to conceive so of the latter, and I will leave the Asserters of this Position to grapple with the Two former, so that this Doctrine is burnt up with the City of *Sodom*.

3. The third and last Instance was that of Gods drowning the World: No doubt but there were Millions of young Infants living in the old World when the flood came and swept away all but *Noah* and his Family, who were but Eight Persons, and yet none but the ungodly perished in that Deluge of Wrath as well as Water, 2 *Pet.* 2. 5. *And spared not the old world, but saved Noah the eighth person, a preacher of Righteousness* [That was, he was a Preacher of the Gospel, wherein is Revealed the Righteousness of Christ unto them which believe unto the saving of their Souls] *bringing in the Flood upon the World of the Ungodly.* And Children were a very great part of the Old World, though it will not be granted by the Men of this Opinion, that they are a part of all Nations which were to be Discipled in *Matth.* 28. 19. And God will save no ungodly Person whatsoever, young or old; and unless their Natures are changed, they are ungodly still, because by Nature we are all so; therefore this Doctrine was drowned also with the Old World.

quoted *Rom.* 5. 14. to corroborate
trange Doctrine: The words are as
*Nevertheless Death Reigned from Adam
 over them that had not sinned after the
 Adams transgression, who is the figure
 as to come.*

Six things to be observed from these
 first is this,

efore the Law of *Moses* took place, it
of Great Darkness and Ignorance.

thstanding that did not Excuse them,
n Temporal Death, nor Eternal; for
faith, *Nevertheless Death Reigned from
es.*

Reigns most where Ignorance and
igneth.

gned over them which had not sinned
ilitude of *Adams* Transgression.

h they did not sin after the similitude
ransgression, yet they were Sinners, or
ld have been said they did not sin

astly, Hence we may observe, That
Figure of *Christ*, who was to come
h.

ving premised these things, I proceed
mething to the Second Observation, as
which our Opponents did lay the most
for the maintaining the Salvation of all
nts, in these words, *Nevertheless Death
 Adam to Moses, even over them that
ned after the similitude of Adams trans-*
ppose we allow them, that this was
Dying Infants only, yet this will not
ind of Relief to this fictitious Doctrine,

Dying

1. *Dying Infants cannot be said to sin after the similitude or likeness of Adams transgression.*

The Reasons are as followeth,

First, There was no Pre-existent Corruption for *Adam* to derive sin from by Nature or Transmutation; for *Adam* was not a Child of Wrath by Nature or Derivation; for God made him upright: But all Persons since the Fall, our Blessed Redeemer only excepted, derives sin from the Loynes of our first Parents.

2. Though Young Infants have all the Seeds of Depraved sinful Nature in them, transmitted to them from the contaminated Loynes of our first Parents, who acquired it from Satan, yet they are not capable of drawing forth those Habits into Actual Transgression; for as *Adams* Transgression did not proceed from Original Corruption in himself, so neither doth the sin of such young Babes proceed from any Actual Transgression, and therefore young Children do not sin after the similitude or likeness of *Adams* Transgression; for *Adam* was guilty of Actual Transgression, but young Babes are only guilty of Original Sin, which makes a vast Dissimilitude.

3. And lastly, Young Infants are not capable of being tempted by Satan to commit actual Transgression, nor of yielding to the Temptations of Satan, as our first Parents did; for they were not only tempted by him, but they yielded unto his Temptation, therefore young Children are not capable of sinning after the similitude of *Adams* Transgression, for the one fell into sin by Temptation, and the other sins by Derivation from the Loynes of our first Parents.

Now pray what can be gathered from this Text of Scripture, to prove this General Redemption and Salvation for all Dying Infants, as they Dream of;

; for though these Dying Infants did not, nor
not sin after the similitude of *Adams* Transgression, but yet they were not free from Original
[Si]n, and that is sufficient to damn any Soul, unless the guilt on't be Removed and Expiated by the
[Ri]ghteousness and Merits of Jesus Christ imputed
[to] their Souls through the Grace of Faith; For
[th]ey are in a state of Unbelief, and therefore
[th]ey must have the Grace of Faith to change that
[St]ate: Do but look into *Rom.* 5. 12. There you
[ha]ve the Malady, and in *verse* 15, there you have
[th]e Remedy: And I pray mind them.

1. The Malady, *Wherefore as by one man sin entred into the world, and Death by sin, and so Death passed upon all Men, for that all have sinned.*

2. Here is the Remedy prescribed in these words, *But not as the offence, so also is the Free Gift, for if through the offence of one many be dead, much more the Grace of God, and the Gift by Grace, which is by one man, Jesus Christ, hath abounded to many.* Verse 16. *And not as it was by one that sinned, so is the Gift, for the Judgment was by one to condemnation, but the Free Gift is of many offences unto Justification.* All men sin and destroy themselves by Nature: For if it were possible for a Man to live to the years of *Methusalah*, and never commit any one act of sin, and dye in a Natural state in which he was conceived and born: He could not be saved, because he is in a State of Wrath, and he is also a Child of Wrath: Man sins and Destroys himself by Nature, but God justifieth and saves by Grace, *Eph.* 2. 8.

3. Said they, All Dying Infants are Saved, but not Elected; which Assertion contradicts the whole current of the Holy Scripture which do run in this Channel, and it thwarts the Eternal Decrees and Methods of God in his predeterminated Council about the Redemption and Salvation

tion of Sinners. Pray mind thefe following Scriptures, and confute them if you can; fo: contradict them I fee you dare.

1. Acts 13. *And as many as were ordained to eternal life believed.*

2. Mark 13. 20. *And except that the Lord had shortned thofe days, no flefh fhould be faved: but fo the elects fake, whom he hath chofen, he hath fhortned the days.*

4. John 10. *But ye believe not, becaufe ye are not of my fheep:* That is, they were not Elected and therefore they did not believe.

5. John 15. *Ye have not chofen me, but I have chofen you,* &c.

6. John 1. 12, 13. *But as many as received him to them gave he power to become the fons of God, even to them that believe on his name.*

This muft not be underftood, as if they received Chrift before he had planted a Spiritual living Principle in them, whereby to inable them to take hold of Chrift, and receive him by Faith for to receive Chrift is to believe in him; for the fame *verfe* tells you fo, *even to them that believe on his name*; and the following *verfe* deftroys all Natural Power and Ability in the Will of Man to receive Chrift, or come to Chrift, except it had been to deftroy and crucifie him, as the Jew did.

Verfe 13. *Which were born, not of blood, nor of the will of the flefh, nor of the will of man, but of God.*

7. Rom. 9. *For the children being not yet born, neither having done any good or evil, that the purpofe of God according to election might ftand. Jacob have I loved, but Efau have I hated. What fhall we fay then? Is there unrighteoufnefs with God? God forbid. So then it is not of him that willeth, nor of him that runneth*

runneth, but of God that sheweth mercy. Therefore hath he mercy on whom he will have mercy, and whom he will, he hardeneth. What if God, willing to shew his wrath, and to make his power known, endureth with much long-suffering the vessels of wrath fitted for destruction: And that he might make known the riches of his glory on the vessels of mercy, which he had afore prepared unto glory? 2 *John* 1. 1. *Jer.* 1. 5. 1 *Pet.* 2. 9. *Tit.* 1. 2. I could produce Multitudes of Scriptures more to confute this Errour, but I think there is Bones enough in them I have named, for all the Free-willers in the World to gnaw upon, until they break all their Holders.

4. There are but two sorts of People in the World, namely, Jews and Gentiles; and all these are made up into two sorts of Vessels, the one to Honour, and the other to Dishonour, one of Mercy, and the other of Wrath, which comprehends all Persons, Young and Old, Saints and Sinners, in the whole World.

Therefore I challenge any Man whatsoever to prove by plain Text of Scripture, That ever any one dying Infant was saved without being Elected. I shall conclude this first part of this Head with that unanswerable Scripture in *Rom.* 11. 5. *Even so then at this present time also there is a remnant according to the election of grace. And if by grace, then it is no more of works: otherwise grace is no more grace. But if it be of works, then it is no more grace: otherwise work is no more work. What then? Israel hath not obtained that which he seeketh for; but the election hath obtained it, and the rest were blinded.*

They thought to be justified and saved by the Works of the Law; but by the Deeds of the Law no Flesh shall be justified; and there is no Salva-

Infants; therefore let him hear what the Holy Ghost faith unto him, and let him take it for his pains, *Rom.* 9. 20, 21. *Nay but O man, who art thou that repliest against God? shall the thing formed say to him that formed it, Why hast thou made me thus? Hath not the potter power over the clay, of the same lump to make one vessel unto honour, and another unto dishonour?*

2. You shall see what monstrous Absurdities this strange Doctrine doth beget.

1. If all dying Infants are saved without being Elected, then Christ's Mystical Body, the Church, must be a monstrous Body: But if all the Members of our Natural Bodies are in God's Book of Creation, before ever we were formed, or fashioned in the Womb, as in *Psal.* 139. 15, 16.

2. How much more then are all the Members of Christ's Mystical Body in God the Father's Book of Eternal Election. But,

3. In the Third place let us observe what kind of Body the Mystical Body of Christ is, and how, and in what manner it is framed and compiled.

1. It is a perfect compleat Body, intire and lacking nothing, *Eph.* 4. 11, 12, 13. *And he gave some, apostles: and some, prophets: and some, evangelists: and some, pastors and teachers; For the perfecting of the saints, for the work of the ministery, for the edifying of the body of Christ: Till we all come in the unity of the faith, and of the knowledge of the Son of God, unto a perfect man, unto the measure of the stature of the fulness of Christ.* Here you see Christ's Body must be a perfect Body, as to measure and degree: For all the Elect of God, both

both Young and Old, muſt come into this Union of Faith, which is the Faith of God's Elect, *Tit.* 1. 1.

2. A Second Scripture is in *Rom.* 12. *For as we have many members in one body, and all members have not the ſame office: So we being many are one body in Chriſt, and every one members one of another.* Here the Apoſtle alludes to the Natural Body of Man, to illuſtrate and deſcribe the Frame and Make of the Myſtical Body of Chriſt; and then he brings it about Emphatically, *So we being many are one body in Chriſt, and every one members one of another.*

3. A Third Scripture is in 1 *Cor.* 10. 17. *For we being many are one bread, and one body: for we are all partakers of that one bread.*

4. The Fourth and laſt Scripture that I ſhall mention, as to the Frame of this Myſtical Body of Chriſt, is in *Heb.* 12. 22, 23, 24. *But ye are come unto mount Sion, and unto the city of the living God, the heavenly Jeruſalem, and to an innumerable company of angels, To the general aſſembly and church of the firſt-born which are written in heaven, and to God the judge of all, and to the ſpirits of juſt men, made perfect, And to Jeſus the mediator of the new covenant, and to the blood of ſprinkling, that ſpeaketh better things then that of Abel.* Here you may obſerve what a ſweet Harmony and Agreement there is between theſe Scriptures; and have given in a full Teſtimony, that the Myſtical Body of Chriſt is one Intire Body, lacking nothing, and that all the Members thereof are united and compact together by Faith, and they are all written in Heaven.

2. And Laſtly, Let us obſerve what kind of Body theſe Gentlemen would make the Myſtical Body of Chriſt to be, that would have all dying

H 2   Infants

Infants to be Members of it, that never were in God's Book of Election.

1. I do positively and solemnly declare, that if it were possible, that one Soul could be saved, either of Old or Young, that is not written in God's Book of Eternal Election, that Christ's Mystical Body would be a monstrous Body, and if so, then what must all these dying Infants that they say are saved, but not Elected, nor chosen of God the Father be, but supernumerous Members? And if so, how many Millions of Members would Christ have in his Mystical Body, which are not in the Book of Life, *viz.* the Book of Election? And what a strange monstrous Body would that be?

2. If there should be but one Member less in Christ's Mystical Body, then there is in God's Eternal Book of Election, then it would be an imperfect Body, and lacking something, whereas it is said, —*perfect, intire, and lacking nothing.*

3. If all dying Infants are saved without being Elected, then will there be more superfluous chance Members in Christ's Mystical Body by Millions, then there will be of Elect true Members, because there have more Children dyed in all Nations and Ages of the World then Adult Believers, perhaps a Thousand to one, and more.

4. In the Fourth and last place, As all the Elect of God, in all Ages and Nations of the World, and of all Sects, and Years, or Dayes, make but one Mystical Body, namely, The Holy Catholick Church, so our Saviour Christ is Married to that Mystical Holy Body: And if any should be saved which were never Elected, then our Saviour Christ would have Two Wives, one by Luck and Chance, and the other by Love and Choice. But we read of but one Spouse, or one Wife,

Wife, that Chrift hath, *Sol.* 4. 8, 9. *Come with me from Lebanon, my spouse,* &c. *Rev.* 19. 7. *Let us be glad and rejoice, and give honour to him: for the marriage of the Lamb is come, and his wife hath made her self ready.* And so in like manner all the Elect, which make but one Spiritual Myftical Body, have but one Husband, *Sol.* 2. 8, 16. *The voice of my beloved! behold, he cometh leaping upon the mountains, skipping upon the hills. My beloved is mine, and I am his: he feedeth among the lilies. Ifa.* 54. 5. *For thy maker is thine husband, (the Lord of hofts is his name:) and thy redeemer the holy One of Ifrael, the God of the whole earth shall he be called.*

Thus you fee there is but one Head and Husband, and but one Wife, one Body, and but one Covenant, in which they all are, which is a Marriage Covenant, and but one Faith, by which this Conjugal Union is made, and but one way to Eternal Life and Salvation for all the Elect of God.

And from hence we may obferve, that it is a very dangerous thing for any Perfon to meafure thefe Profound Myfteries with the fhort Line of corrupt carnal Senfe and Reafon, and to Affert, that God cannot be Juft unlefs he doth fave all dying Infants: Therefore let this be a feafonable Word of Caution unto all *Antipredeftinators* as well as to others.

4. Said they, *All dying Infants are faved, but none are Regenerated and born again:* Which contradicts our Saviour Chrift's own Words, *John* 3. *Jefus anfwered and faid unto him, Verily verily I fay unto thee, Except a man be born again, he cannot fee the kingdom of God.* John 1. 13. *Which were born, not of bloud, nor of the will of the flesh, nor of the will of man, but of God.* 1 John 5. 18. *We know that whofoever is born of God finneth not, but he that*

H 3 *is*

is begotten of God, keepeth himself, and that wicked one toucheth him not. The Devil, who is that wicked one, cannot so touch him by all his Skill, nor so allure him by all his Baits and Stratagems, as to bring him back again into his Kingdome of Darkness, because he is begotten of God. A Child that is born into the World may as soon be reduced by Annihilation into nothing, its Original, because he is kept by the Mighty Power of God, through Faith, unto Salvation, (1 *Pet.* 3. 4, 5.) which is that Vital Principle that God alone by his own Right Hand doth plant in all the Souls of the Heirs of Salvation: Therefore he that is born of God cannot fall totally from Grace; and he that is not born of God hath no Grace to fall from; and all the Seed of the first *Adam* are Children of Wrath by Nature, and except they are Regenerated, and their Natures changed, they cannot be saved; they must be made Partakers of the Divine Nature: So that without Regeneration there can be no Salvation for any of the Race of Fallen Man. Thus you see this Errour is also confuted.

5. Said they, *All dying Infants are saved without the Grace of Faith:* To which I thus Answer, If they are saved without Faith, then they must be saved by Works: Pray mind the Apostle in *Rom.* 11. 6. *And if by grace, then it is no more of works: otherwise grace is no more grace. But if it be of works, then it is no more grace: otherwise work is no more work.* What think ye on't now? Here it is plain from the Words of the Apostle, That the Salvation of Young or Old, is either of Gods Mercy, or Mans Merit; but it cannot be by the latter, therefore it must be by the former, (*Luke* 17. 10.) and without Faith it is impossible to please God; *Rom.* 4. 5. *But to him that worketh not*

not, but believeth on him that justifieth the ungodly, his faith is counted for righteousness. But Mr. *H. C.* faith in Page 12. That *none are Christ's Disciples but such as take up his Cross, and follow him:* Ergo, Infants are not Disciples, and so no visible Members of a Gospel Church. By the same Argument he doth exclude them from Heaven, and Eternal Salvation; and indeed there is no Argument they can use to exclude them from the one, but doth necessarily exclude them from the other; for they are visible Church Members, as being a Part of their Parents, who are visible Church Members, and being the Covenant Seed; but he should have compared Scripture with Scripture. What tho' Elect dying Infants are not capable of taking up Christ's Cross, and following him in Sufferings and Persecutions? Yet they are capable of following him in the Regeneration, *Mat.* 19. 28. And pray how did *Nicodemus* follow Christ when he came to our Saviour by Night by stealth? He did not follow him with his Cross. And how did those follow Christ of whom it is said in *John* 12. *Nevertheless, among the chief rulers also, many believed on him; but because of the Pharisees they did not confess him, lest they should be put out of the synagogue.* These were Disciples, yet they did not follow Christ with his Cross, but shunn'd it: And is not a Young Infant, that hath but Habitual Faith, as capable to follow Christ in the Regeneration, as these Adult Persons were? For if they are united to Christ, then they must follow him, and Faith is the uniting Grace, *Eph.* 4. *Till we all come in the unity of the faith, and of the knowledge of the Son of God, unto a perfect man, unto the measure of the stature of the fulness of Christ.*

Thus you see how all the Elect of God comes to be united, *viz.* Christ is by Faith; therefore as without

out Faith it is impoſſible to pleaſe Goc
out Faith there can be no Union with (
without Union with him there can be n
by him, *John* 15. 5. *John* 6. 40. And ſo
mental Errour of ſaving dying Infants
Grace of Faith is condemned to be me

6. Said they, *All dying Infants are
not ſanctified, becauſe* (ſaid they) *the Dec
took away the Guilt of Original Sin fro
Infants:* To which I Anſwer, This ca
true, unleſs all dying Infants are El
they will not allow, that any ſuch Cl
Elected; for all that are Elected ſhall
fied; and if you look into the Holy
you ſhall find Election, Salvation, Sal
and Faith, all four joined together t
Spirit, in 2 *Theſſ.* 2. 13. And what
joined together let not vain Men labc
aſunder: The Blood of Chriſt cleanſe
ſin; but to imagine that any ſhall be
out being ſanctified, is a vain Imagin
without Holineſs no Man ſhall ſee the
cauſe no unclean thing ſhall enter in
Heb. 10. *By the which will we are ſancti
the offering of the body of Jeſus Chriſt o*
That was, for all the Elect of God:
Paſſeover is ſacrificed for us. Here is tl
in Goſpel-times, which is the Eſſence o
over, though the Form thereof is aboli
5. 7. Thus you ſee this Errour is alſo (

7. They Aſſerted, That *all dying
ſaved without being in a State of Grace*
they) *Chriſt by his Death purchaſed E
and Salvation for them all; and ſo thej
through his Righteouſneſs:* But without
you ſee none of them will allow that C
capable of receiving the Grace of Faitl
Ri

Righteousness of Christ is applicable to none but God's Elect, Old or Young, and that through the Instrumentality of Faith. This is the Truth my Soul relies upon for Eternal Life and Salvation; and had I Ten Thousand Souls more, I would venture them all on this Bottom; *Eph.* 2. 8. *For by Grace are ye saved, through Faith; and that not of your selves: it is the gift of God.* Faith is the Gift of God, and Repentance is the Gift of God, and Christ is the Gift of God, and the Holy Ghost is the Gift of God, and Sanctification is the Work of God's Spirit in the Soul: But the *Anabaptists*, by their Carnal Reason, will allow God to bestow these Gifts upon none but Adult Persons: So that you see this Errour is also confuted.

8. They Asserted, That *all dying Infants are saved, but not in the Covenant of Grace:* To which I Answer thus,

1. There are but two Covenants, in which are contained all the Persons in the whole World, Old and Young, Saints and Sinners: (1.) The one is the Covenant of Grace; And (2.) the other is the Covenant of Works; And all those that are in the Covenant of Grace are safe, and not one Soul of them can be lost: (2.) All that live and dye in the Covenant of Works can never be saved. And,

2. Those Two Covenants were in being before *Abraham*'s Time, and in his Time, and are still in being, and ever will be to the End of the World; and these are the same Two Covenants which the Apostle sets forth in that Allegory, by *Abraham*'s Two Sons, in *Gal.* 4. *For it is written, that Abraham had two sons; the one by a bondmaid, the other by a free-woman. But he who was of the bond-woman, was born after the flesh: but he*

of the free-woman was by promise. Here the Carnal and Spiritual Seed of *Abraham* are represented. *Which things are an allegory ; for these are the two covenants ; the one from the mount Sinai, which gendereth to bondage, which is Agar, For this Agar is mount Sinai in Arabia, and answereth to Jerusalem which now is, and is in bondage with her children.* This is the Church of God that was then in persecution by those of *Mount Sinai*; for you see the Apostle spake in the Present Tense. *But Jerusalem which is above, is free, which is the mother of us all.* The Church Triumphant in Glory hath none of *Agars* Seed or Off-spring in it, but she is free from all such; there is none but the Children of the Free-woman there; in that Church there is neither Persecutor nor Hypocrite, which are the two Grand Enemies the Church of Christ hath in the World. But all that are of the Free-woman, namely, the Covenant of Grace, shall be saved; and there is no Salvation to be had for any others, whether they are dying Infants, or Adult Persons: And thus you see this Errour also confuted.

9. And Lastly, That which seems as strange as all the rest is, that these very Persons, at the same time, do hold the Doctrine of Predestination, and that God's Grace is Free, and Eternal Election, which contradicts all their foregoing Positions and Doctrines; for they will not allow Children to have any share in it.

Thus you see an Errour in Judgment cannot live and subsist alone; and that Soul that goeth a Mile with an Errour, it will soon compel him to go with him twain. First, they deny the Infant Seed of Believers to have a Right to the Ordinance of Baptism, and to maintain this Error, all these Errors and Absurdities aforesaid, and

more

more, muſt be Lifted in their Service to uphold it.

And now I am come to Treat with my Friend of *Rocheſter*, that was ſo kind to ſend me a Letter. Sir, I have carefully peruſed it, and I find you have ſaid as much to the purpoſe as all the reſt, and wiſh as well to your Cauſe as the beſt of them, and yet all you have ſaid is to very little purpoſe, unleſs it be to contradict all the reſt; but yet though I obſerve you differ from all the reſt very much, and in ſeveral things, yet I find that you aim at the ſame thing in the Maine; for you do alſo meaſure the Profound Myſteries of the Covenant by the Carnal Rule of corrupt Senſe, and Humane Reaſon, even as *Nicodemus* did the Doctrine of Regeneration, *John* 3. 3, 4. or as the Jews did in *John* 6. 52.

1. Say you, *I am troubled at your Reflections upon ſome of Mr.* H. C's. *Notions in his Book*; But I obſerve you do confeſs that you never ſaw it: This is a very Strange Faculty that many of your Opinion have, that you will Juſtifie thoſe Books of your own People, though you never ſaw them, and alſo judge and condemn thoſe Books that are ſet forth by Men of our Principle, though they never ſaw, nor heard them Read: And what ſaith *Solomon* of thoſe that judge a Man before they hear him? But you have Avouched him to be found in the Fundamentals of Religion; but how can a Man be ſaid to be found in the Fundamentals of Religion, that denies that Elect dying Infants are capable of receiving the Grace of Faith, and yet owns they are ſaved? And if they are ſaved without faith, then are they ſaved by works, *Rom.* 11. 6. Where is your found Man now? For if this

this be not a Fundamental Errour, Pray what is ?

2. You say you may submit to all my Queries about Infants being saved dying in their Infancy, or Adult Persons, who are the Elect of God: Then say I, They have a Right to the Ordinance of Baptism, and you ought to have submitted to that also.

3. Say you, *We have no other way for saving Infants, or Adult Persons, but by the Death, Blood, and Merits of Jesus Christ: There is no other way, as I know of.* No, neither any of our Opinion; but the Books of those of your own Opinion, you see contradict you, both Mr. *H. C.* and *B. K.* But Sir, by your Good Favour, you your self have left out the Principal Instrumental Ingredient in Mans Salvation, namely, the Grace of Faith, without which it is impossible for any Person, Young or Old, to be saved, and the Reason is, Because *without Faith it is impossible to please God*; for all Mankind, before Conversion, are in a State of Unbelief and Impenitency, therefore they must have the Grace of Faith, which is the opposite Grace to the Sin of Unbelief, to change them: But before you said, That he, or she, that believes not, shall be damned. So that if these two Assertions of yours may be joined together, then if Adult Persons are saved by Faith in the Righteousness and Merits of Jesus Christ, so are dying Infants also: So that you and I agree in this; for you say, you have no other way for saving Infants, or Adult Persons, but by the Death, Blood, and Merits of Jesus Christ, &c. Then Infants and Adult Persons are saved in one, and the same way; so that we have no more to do, but to inquire what that way is, wherein the Adult are saved, and the Controversie is ended. All Adult Believers are saved by Faith in our Lord Jesus Christ

Christ, *Acts* 16. *Sirs, what must I do to be saved? And they said, Believe on the Lord Jesus Christ, and thou shalt be saved, and thy house.* John 6. 35, 40.

4. Say you, *Neither doth God break Covenant with his People; but he holds that firm to the End, without any alteration.* You see, that I am of the same Judgment; but Mr. *H. C.* whom you say is found in the Fundamentals of Religion, faith, That the Covenant of Peculiarity made with *Abraham,* in *Gen.* 17. 7. is Repealed, and Taken up by the Roots: But if God did not Break, nor Alter the Covenant, then are the Infant Seed of Believers as much in it now, as ever the Infant Seed of Believers were under the *Mosaick* Law, and have as good a Right unto all the Priviledges thereof, as ever the Jews Children had, unless it can be proved, that ever these Young Babes have broken Covenant with God themselves, by any Actual Transgression, under the Gospel, and so sinned themselves out of Covenant: If they did, pray where, and when was it?

But if God hath not Broken his Covenant, nor altered it, nor the Infant Seed of Believers themselves Broken it, then are they still in Covenant with God.

5. Say you, *That Faith that fits a Person for one Ordinance fits him for another.*

And (faith Mr. *H. C.*) *we do Assert Infants may be fit for the Kingdom of God, as our Lord hath said, and yet not Qualified for Gospel Ordinances.* But I do not know where our Lord hath said it, nor he neither.

But I suppose you mean, that Faith that fits Infants for Baptism, fits them for the Lords Table: But I have confuted this Notion in my former Book sufficiently already, to which I must Refer
the

the Reader, and ask this one single Question, *viz*. Did that Grace which did fit the Covenant Seed of Believers at Eight Days old for the Ordinance of Circumcision, fit them for the Passeover? It did give them a Remote Right unto it; even so doth that Grace, that fits the Infant Seed of Believers for the Ordinance of Baptism, give them a Remote Right, though not a Meetness for the Ordinance of Commemoration of Christ our Passover, that was sacrificed for us. Whatever Priviledge the Infant Seed of Believers enjoyed under the Law, the Infant Seed of Believers enjoy now under the Gospel, in a better Dress; for God hath as much Love for the Infant Seed of Believers now, as ever he had under the Law, *Heb*. 9. 14, 22, 23, 24.

6. You Grant, That Children may have Faith in the Habit, but not in the Act, and therefore (say you) they are of no use in the Church.

Sir, You began well, and who did hinder you? seeing you did thus begin in the Spirit, that you should end in the Flesh, namely, in Carnal Reason, and Humane Policy? How can this be, that Children that have Habitual Faith are of no use in the Church? When our Saviour Christ saith, *Of such is the kingdom of God*. which is the Church; and the Apostle saith by Allusion, that there are several sorts of Vessels in the House of God, in 2 *Tim*. 2. 20, 21. But it is Christ by his Spirit that doth purge and sanctifie them, and make them Meet Vessels of Honour, fit for their Masters use: *Heb*. 10. 10, 14, 16, 17.

2. You may as well query, What use are Children of in a Family? Are they not for Delight and Complacency, and to hold up the Name of their Father? So are these Children of the like use in the House of God; they hold up the Name
.of

of God; for wherever there is Habitual Faith, there is the Name of God Recorded in that Soul.

3. As Parents keep Nurses and Servants to attend upon Children, and are at great Charge with them, and receive no visible profit by them; Why even so Gods Spirit doth Nurse the Graces of these Young Disciples, and his Holy Angels are Servants unto them; for they are Heirs of Salvation; *Heb*. 1. *But to which of the angels said he at any time, Sit on my right hand, until I make thine enemies thy footstool? Are they not all ministring spirits, sent forth to minister for them who shall be heirs of salvation?* And God is not profited by the Service of any of his People.

4. We find that our Saviour did Love, Bless, and own the Children of believing Parents to be of the Church, *Mat.* 19. 14. And pray mind that Word of Christ, which should be a Caution to all you Infant Despisers, *Mat.* 18. 10. *Take heed that ye despise not one of these little ones; for I say unto you, that in heaven their angels do always behold the face of my Father which is in heaven.*

5. Pray do but observe what an Honour Christ put upon Children in his Answer to those carnal, despising Priests and Scribes, in *Mat.* 21. 15, 16. *And when the chief priests and scribes saw the wonderful things that he did, and the children crying in the temple, and saying, Hosanna to the son of David; they were sore displeased, And said unto him, Hearest thou what these say,* &c. Here you may observe Two Things: (1.) They were sorely inraged against the Lord Jesus Christ, because the People with Loud Acclamations confessed Christ to be the Messiah, and for this his Enemies were inraged against him, and by way of Derision said, *Hearest thou what these say?* As if they should have said,

Hearest

Hearest thou what these Little Children say? They praise thee in the Temple; but what do their praising of thee signifie? For they are of no use in the Temple, or Church of God: But our Saviour's Answer to them may be a very seasonable Rebuke to this Clamour, that is much of the same kind with the Chief Priests and Scribes in that Day, in *verse* 16. *And Jesus said unto them, Have ye never read, Out of the mouth of babes and sucklings thou hast perfected praise?*

1. What an Excellent Character did our Saviour Christ give of the Praise of these Little Children, *viz. perfected praise*; and pray mind the reason of it in *Psal.* 8. 2. *Out of the mouth of babes and sucklings hast thou ordained strength, because of thine enemies, that thou mightest still the enemy and the avenger.*

2. Here you see Children were of great use in the Church of God, both under the Law and Gospel: For what greater use can there be in the Church, of any Members thereof, then to render perfect Praise unto God? Therefore pray Sir, let me advise you, that you never open your Mouth more, whilst you live, to ask such a Carnal, unchristian Question as this, *viz.* What use are Young Children of in the Church?

8. Say you, *But as for Circumcision, a Seal of Righteousness, that was a clear Command to Abraham, and his Seed at Eight Days old,* Gen. 17. *but not one word in the Gospel for baptizing or sprinkling of Infants.*

1. I do own that Circumcision was a Seal of Righteousness, and a clear Command to *Abraham*, and his Seed at Eight Days old, and I must add, that this Seal was one of the Seals of *Abraham's* Covenant,

Covenant, and therefore, say I, the Children of believing Parents, now under the Gospel, being in the very same Covenant, have a Right to the Seal of Righteousness, which belongeth as much to the Covenant now, as ever it did belong to it under the Law, or else this Seal of Righteousness is lost; but that can never be lost, nor dissolved, because the Covenant which God made with *Abraham* is an Everlasting Covenant, and can never be Dissolved, nor Repealed, and so is the Seal, or Token thereof, *Gen.* 17. 7, 11, 13. And,

2. Pray what is the Reason, that we have *Abraham* so often mentioned in the Gospel, but to Assure us, that all that are saved since that Covenant was made with *Abraham*, are saved in that Covenant?

3. Christ the Mediator of the Covenant, took not on him the Nature of Angels, but the Seed of *Abraham*; And what is the Reason the Apostles mention *Abraham*, and the Seed of *Abraham*, and the Blessing of *Abraham* coming upon the Gentiles, and the Promises which belong to the Covenant of *Abraham*, and that *Abraham* is the Father of the Believing Gentiles, and all this in Gospel-Times? *Rom.* 4. 8, 9, 10, 11, 12, 13. How came *Abraham* to be Heir of the World, and the Gentiles to be Fellow-Heirs with the Jews, which were his Natural Seed? Therefore *Abraham*'s Covenant is not abolished; but stands fast, and fixed, and the Seal of Righteousness also, *Gal.* 3. 13, 14. *Eph.* 3. 6. *Acts* 2. 38, 39. Now all these Scriptures, which are the Gospel of that Command which God gave unto *Abraham* for Circumcision, is sufficient Ground and Authority for Christian Believers to Baptize all their Children in their Infancy, it being no where forbid, nor their Children ever cast out of the Covenant, unless the Covenant

nant hath loft that Seal of Righteoufnefs, which doth principally belong to Infants, and not to the Adult at all, after it had Initiated the Head of the Family into the Covenant; for after the firft Inftitution of Circumcifion it was Death for any Jew not to be circumcifed in his Infancy, *Gen.* 17. 12, 14. So Adult Believers have nothing to do with the Ordinance of Baptifm, after the firft Inftitution, or Plantation of the Gofpel in a Family, unlefs it be fuch Perfons whofe Parents unbelief deprived them of it in their Infancy; fuch ought to be baptized when they are Adult, upon the Confeffion of their Faith; but Baptifme of Right is devolved upon the Infant Seed of Believers only, as Circumcifion did; and therefore the Baptifm of the *Anabaptifts* cannot be good, and that principally for thefe Four Reafons following,

1. Becaufe they difown the Covenant God made with *Abraham*, in which the very Foundation for Baptifme was laid. Let them find out any other Foundation for it if they can: For that Covenant is founded upon Chrift himfelf, *Gal.* 3. 13, 14. And the Apoftle in the 15th. *verfe*, to confirm the Stability of the Covenant there, fhews us by illuftration, that if a covenant that is between Man and Man about their own private Affairs, ought to be kept Inviolably and Unalterably; much more fhall the Covenant which God made with *Abraham*, which is in Chrift, be kept Inviolable and Unalterable. Pray read the Gofpel, and underftand it, and not thus abufe our Covenant Mercy.

2. Becaufe they baptize the Adult Seed of Believers, that were baptized in their Infancy as they ought to be.

3. Their Baptifm cannot be good becaufe they deny it to their own Seed and Off-fpring, when as the Covenant is made to Believers and their

their Seed: So that either they are no Believers themselves, or else they Reprobate their own Children.

4. And Lastly, Their Baptism cannot be good, because their Principle is to baptize Adult Believers, but not their Seed, which is to baptize but a part of the Believer, whereas they should not only baptize him, but all of him: So that their Baptism it self is but a counterfeit Baptism.

9. And Lastly, You put Three Queries to me, 1. Whether Children are in the Covenant of Grace Absolutely or Conditionally? 2. Whether that can be an Ordinance of Christ, for which there is neither Precept nor Example, &c. 3. And Lastly, Whether in Matter of meer positive Right, such as Baptism is, we ought not to keep expresly and punctually to the Revealed Will of the Law-giver? But where do you find any express Command for the Infant-Seed of Believers to stay until they are Adult to be baptized, after the first Plantation of the Gospel in Families; for whatever the Conditions were, which God made with *Abraham* and his Seed, both Spiritual and Carnal, are the same now unto Believers and their Seed, both Spiritual and Carnal, being in the very same Covenant as they were. But I have Answered these Queries already, and you, your own self, by allowing all my Queries in my former Book to be found and good, have Answered them. And thus we may see how all those Men, that I have here been Treating with, do differ one from another, though all of them do hold particular Election.

In the last place to conclude, this Opinion of the *Anabaptists* is very prejudicial upon many accounts you see, and many Errors and Absurdities

attend

attend it; and among the reft it doth mightily hinder Union in Judgment and Affection.

1. It hinders Union in Judgment, which is a fin, becaufe the Scripture faith, in 1 *Cor.* 1. 10. *Now I befeech you; Brethren, by the Name of our Lord Jefus Chrift, that ye all speak the same thing, and that there be no divisions among you; but that ye be perfectly joyned together in the same mind, and in the same judgment.*

2. It hinders Union in Love and Affection, *Phil.* 2. *Fulfil ye my Joy, that ye be like minded, having the same love, being of one accord, of one mind.*

3. It hinders Union in Joy and Confolation, *Rom.* 5. *Now the God of patience and confolation grant you, to be like minded one towards another, according to Chrift Jefus, that ye may with one mind, and one mouth, glorifie God,* &c.

Rom. 12. *Rejoyce with them that Rejoyce, be of the same mind one towards another.*

4. It hinders Union in the Worfhip of God, for we ought to ferve the Lord with one confent.

5. It hinders Union in Faith, and Edifying the Churches of Jefus Chrift, *Eph.* 4. 11, 12, 13, 14.

6. And laftly, It doth confequentially hinder the fulfilling of thefe Prophefies, *Zeph.* 3. 9. *For then will I turn to the People a pure Language, that they may all call upon the Name of the Lord, to ferve him with one confent,* Zech. 14. 9. *And the Lord shall be King over all the Earth: in that day shall there be one Lord, and his name one.*

Thus you fee, thefe Differences as flight as fome Men make of them, are very pernicious and mifchievous; It renders us juft like a Company of Men that are building a large Edifice, that when one hath laid the Foundation, another comes and takes it up, and lays it another way; and another comes, and he takes it up again, and will
have

e of the causes of Division in *Heb.* 6.
ing the principles of the Doctrines of
go on unto perfection, not laying again
of Repentance from dead works, and
is God ; of the Doctrine of Baptisme,
on *of hands,* nd *of the Resurrection of*
of eternal judgment.
f the *Anabaptists* are concerned in all
l of them are concerned in most of
:y are laying a new Foundation for
om Dead Works, and Faith towards
left Dying Infants, as I have shewn.
ill be apt to say it is not convenient
t such things as these are at this jun-
; it will but create Divisions and
nong us ; to which I Answer in the
at it will not, but it will rather tend
Affection : For what is the cause of
Errours in Judgment ; therefore if
:o remove the Cause, the Effect will
: can never be united in Affection ,
is differ in Judgment, it is impossi-
Incongruous ; for saith the Scrip-
walk together except they are agreed ?
ation carryeth a strong Negation
of it : Fire and Water may as well
and dwell together comparatively :
sad Experience been our School-
; many years in this point ? Thus I
h you all for the present, and my
and Prayer to God is that we may
) the Standard of the Lord Jesus
Unity of the Faith of God's Elect.
And

And thus you see I have fully answer'd all their Carnal Allegations and Arguments, and clearly vindicated my former Book, Intituled, *An Antidote to prevent the Prevalency of Anabaptisme from that Fallacious Assertion of being a Counterfeit.* And so my Beloved, *Fare ye well all in the Lord.*

POSTSCRIPT.

ALthough I have thus written concerning the *Anabaptists*, and proved their Congregations to be no Churches, and their Baptism to be but counterfeit, and their Opinion Sacrilegious, in that they Rob the Church of Christ of her Treasure, *viz.* All the Infant-Seed of Believers, nevertheless I do believe that there are many good People among them; but they are such, as are better than that Opinion; for I know how to distinguish between Persons and their Opinion, though Mr. H. C. could not; but instead of that he falls upon my Person, in his pretended Answer to my Book, which Answer was a meer Complication of Calumniation, profound Confidence, Ignorance, wrong Topicks, false *Mediums*, perversion of Scriptures, and Non-sence; and some of that Opinion have another way of Answering Books, that detect their Principles, and that is by giving them an Ill Name, *viz.* In saying, It is a silly Thing, not worth Reading, nor Answering: But if it be a Book in favour of their own Principles, though it be stuffed with never so many Errours and Absurdities, they cry it up to a Degree of Infallibility, although they never read the one, nor saw the other; and of both these Practices I my self am not without some Experience, which

doth

oth something border upon that kind of Practice, which is condemned by *Solomon* in *Prov.* 17. 15. *He that justifieth the wicked, and he that condemneth the just, even they both are an abomination to the Lord.* Indeed this is counted good Policy amongst the *Papists*; but me-thinks it should not be so among *Protestants*: But it may be some of our own Prinple, that are either ignorant of our Principles, or not faithful to them, will be apt to say, that I am too harsh; but is this harsher in me, than was in them to Assert, That our Churches are unbaptized *Babylonish* Churches, and our sprinkling of Infants in Baptism is a Relique of Antichrist; which is false? Pray what is the *English* of this? Is it not to unchurch us? But that which I have charged them with, I have sufficiently proved; for both their pretended Churches, and Baptism, are upon wrong Foundations, and their opinion is but a Bone of Antichrist, that hath been thrown in among us, to divide us, and it is pity but it should be thrown back at him again. Now the difference between their Principles and ours are not so indifferent as that both can be right; for if they be in the Right, then we are in the wrong: But I have proved the contrary, and this makes those *Anabaptists*, that are best acquainted with their own Principles refuse to have Christian Communion with us: For either they are no True Church, or we are not, whoever sayeth the contrary: For we do believe, that our Church State is in the Covenant which God made with *Abraham*, which Covenant is Christ, *Isa.* 42. 6. God gave Christ to be a Covenant to the People, (they were the Jews,) and for a Light to the Gentiles; and the Foundation of our Baptism is in *Abraham's* Covenant: But this Covenant is not the Foundation of the *Anabaptists* Church,

nor

nor Baptifme; for they deny the very Being of that Covenant, and faye, that it was Diffolved and plucked up by the Roots at the Incarnation and Crucifiction of our Saviour Chrift; but that is falfe; for our Saviour Chrift did ratifie and confirm that Covenant at his Coming and Incarnation, and Crucifiction, *Dan.* 9. 26. *And after threefcore and two weeks fhall Meffiah be cut off, but not for himfelf,* &c. Verfe 27. *And he fhall confirm the covenant with many for one week:* (that was for all the Elect,) *and in the midft of the week he fhall caufe the facrifice and the oblation to ceafe:* And this made *Abraham* rejoice to fee Chrift Day, *John* 8. 56. *Your Father Abraham rejoiced to fee my day: and he faw it, and was glad.* So that it is impoffible for their Churches to be Right, and True Churches, and ours too; for if they be Right, then we are wrong: But we are upon Covenant Ground, both with a refpect to the Foundation of the Church, and the Ordinance of Baptifme, which is the Door thereof: Therefore they are in the wrong, and we in the right.

● *F I N I S.*

A D V E R T I S E M E N T.

THE Book Intituled, *An Antidote to prevent the Prevalency of Anabaptifme,* is to be Sold at *Nathaniel Holliers,* in *Leaden-Hall-Street,*near *Lime-ftreet-*End, and at *William Chandlers* in the *Poultrey,*and at *Samuel Norcuts* at *Stepney,*and at *William Wingods* in *Kings-ftreet,* *Wapping,* and at *James Wrights* in *Shadwell,* near the Church, and at the Authours, *Gyles Shute* in *Limehoufe.* The Price ftitcht, Six Pence.

www.ingramcontent.com/pod-product-compliance
Lightning Source LLC
Chambersburg PA
CBHW032137160426
43197CB00008B/684